Python Excel External Data Sources

Integrate and Analyze Data from Any Source Seamlessly

Bryan Singer

2

3

Disclaimer

The book titled "**Python Excel External Data Sources: Integrate and Analyze Data from Any Source Seamlessly**" by **Bryan Singer** is intended for informational purposes only. The content provided herein is of a technical nature and is designed to offer guidance and insight into integrating and analyzing data using Python and Excel.

While every effort has been made to ensure the accuracy and reliability of the information presented in this book, it is provided "as is" without warranty of any kind, either express or implied.

Furthermore, the author does not guarantee that the methods and practices described will lead to specific outcomes or results. The book may include references to third-party products, services, or websites, which are provided for convenience and informational purposes only.

Discover Other Books in the Series

"Python for Excel Automation: Advanced techniques, complex Excel tasks"

"Python for Excel Data Analysis: Advanced Techniques, Automate Tasks"

"Python Excel for SQL: Efficiently Importing Excel Data with Panda"

"Python Excel Macros Scripts: Revolutionize Your Excel with Python-Powered Macros"

"Python Excel Dataframes: Advanced CSV Reading and Writing"

"Python Excel Cloud Online Tools: Learn How Python Can Transform Your Excel Experience in the Cloud"

"Python Excel Custom Report Generation: Creating Stunning Custom Reports with Ease"

Introduction

Welcome to the transformative world of "**Python Excel External Data Sources: Integrate and Analyze Data from Any Source Seamlessly.**"

This book is your definitive guide to harnessing the power of Python to enhance your Excel capabilities, turning a popular spreadsheet tool into a powerhouse of data integration and analysis.

Whether you're a seasoned Python programmer, a web developer, a student, or someone passionate about the endless possibilities of Python for Excel, this book is tailored specifically for you.

Imagine a world where you can effortlessly pull data from any external source—be it databases, web APIs, or even real-time data streams—and seamlessly integrate it into your Excel workbooks. The possibilities are truly endless, and the potential impact on your productivity and analytical capabilities is immense.

In today's data-driven world, the ability to effectively manage and analyze diverse data sets is a game-changer. This book is designed to equip you with the skills and knowledge needed to break free from the constraints of traditional data handling methods.

Chapter 1: The Power of Integrating Excel with External Data Sources

Microsoft Excel, long celebrated for its spreadsheet capabilities, transcends its traditional role through integration with external data sources. This chapter explores the significance of this integration, the various external data sources available, and the immense value it brings to businesses and individuals alike.

The Evolution of Excel

Excel has evolved from a simple calculation tool into a robust platform for data analysis and visualization. While its built-in functions and features are powerful, the real game-changer comes from the ability to connect Excel with external data sources. With organizations generating vast amounts of data daily—from customer transactions to social media interactions—Excel's integration capabilities enable users to harness this data effectively.

Understanding External Data Sources

External data sources can be categorized into several types:

Databases: Relational databases (like SQL Server, MySQL, and Oracle) and NoSQL databases (like MongoDB) provide structured data that can be pulled into Excel for detailed analysis.

Web Data: Excel can connect to live data from websites and APIs, allowing users to import real-time information like stock prices, weather updates, and social media analytics.

Cloud Services: Platforms such as Google Sheets,

Salesforce, and various CRM systems house critical data. Excel can connect to these cloud services to consolidate and analyze information in one place.

Spreadsheets: Users can also pull data from other spreadsheets, whether on local drives or shared through cloud storage solutions.

Business Intelligence Tools: Integration with tools like Power BI and Tableau can enhance visual analytics capabilities, allowing users to create more impactful dashboards and presentations.

The Business Impact of Integration

Integrating Excel with external data sources elevates its utility in numerous ways: ### 1. Enhanced Accuracy

Manual data entry is prone to errors, which can lead to faulty analyses. By pulling in data directly from reliable sources, organizations can ensure higher accuracy. This minimizes the risk of miscalculations and enhances trust in the data-driven decisions made.

2. Real-Time Insights

Real-time data feeds empower users to make timely decisions. For example, if a company tracks sales performance, integrating sales data from an external database allows decision-makers to respond quickly to shifts in consumer behavior or market trends.

3. Comprehensive Analysis

By aggregating data from multiple sources, users can gain a holistic view of their business environment. Integrating customer feedback data with sales trends, for instance, can help businesses identify which products resonate most with consumers.

4. Improved Collaboration

Integration fosters seamless collaboration between teams. By connecting to shared external data sources, team members can work with the same set of information, ensuring consistency and reducing silos that often hamper productivity.

5. Automation of Processes

When data flows automatically from external sources into Excel, repetitive tasks are minimized. Automation streamlines efforts, allowing analysts to focus on interpretation and strategy rather than data entry.

How to Integrate Excel with External Data Sources
Step 1: Identifying Your Data Needs

Before diving into integration, it is crucial to clearly define what data is necessary for your analysis. Understanding your objectives will guide you in selecting the appropriate external sources.

Step 2: Establishing Connections

Excel offers various methods for connecting to data sources:

Data Connection Wizard: Excel provides a comprehensive wizard for linking to databases and other sources.

Power Query: This powerful tool within Excel allows users to extract, transform, and load data from a wide range of sources. Power Query is particularly useful for cleaning data and preparing it for analysis.

APIs: For modern web services, Excel can call APIs to retrieve live data. Familiarity with API documentation is essential for smooth integration.

Step 3: Data Refresh Strategy

Establish a refresh strategy that determines how frequently you want your external data to update within Excel. Real-time data might need continuous updates, while less critical information can be refreshed at set intervals.

Step 4: Analyzing Data

Once integrated, utilize Excel's features—pivot tables, charts, functions, and macros—to analyze the gathered information. Explore different visualization techniques to transform raw data into meaningful insights.

Step 5: Sharing Results

Create dashboards and reports in Excel that convey your findings effectively to stakeholders. The collaborative features within Excel and its integration with platforms like Microsoft Teams make sharing and presenting data seamless.

The power of integrating Excel with external data sources cannot be overstated. It enhances accuracy, provides real-time insights, allows for comprehensive analysis, and fosters collaboration within teams. As organizations continue to navigate the complexities of large data sets, leveraging Excel's integration capabilities will be a key differentiator in driving success. In the chapters that follow, we will delve deeper into specific integrations, explore case studies, and uncover strategies for maximizing the potential of this powerful tool in various domains.

Installing Required Python Libraries for Excel

As the use of Python in data analysis and manipulation continues to grow, leveraging its power to interact with Excel spreadsheets has become increasingly essential for data professionals, analysts, and anyone looking to automate their data workflows. This chapter will guide you through the installation of the necessary Python libraries that facilitate seamless interaction with Excel files, helping you streamline your processes effectively.

Understanding the Importance of Python Libraries for Excel

Python provides a robust ecosystem of libraries that allow users to perform a multitude of tasks with Excel files, including reading, writing, and manipulating data. Some of the most popular libraries in this domain include:

Pandas: A powerful library for data manipulation and analysis, providing extensive data structures and functions to work with structured data.

OpenPyXL: A library to read and write Excel 2010 xlsx/xlsm/xltx/xltm files.

XlsxWriter: A library for creating Excel files, aimed at writing data, formatting cells, and adding charts.

PyWin32: Python extensions for Windows that provide access to many of the Windows APIs, enabling control of Excel applications.

Understanding the strengths of each library will empower you to choose the right tools for your specific tasks.

Prerequisites for Installation

Before diving into the installation process, ensure that you

14

have Python installed on your system. It is generally recommended to use the latest version of Python, which you can download from the official Python website [python.org](https://www.python.org/).

To verify the installation of Python, open your command line interface (CLI) and run:

```bash
python --version
``` or

```bash
python3 --version
```

This command should return the current version of Python installed on your machine. If Python is not installed, follow the instructions provided on the website to complete the installation.

Setting Up a Virtual Environment

While not strictly necessary, it is highly advisable to work within a virtual environment. This practice isolates your project dependencies and ensures that you avoid version conflicts between different packages. Here's how to create and activate a virtual environment:

Create a new virtual environment:
```bash
python -m venv myenv
```

Activate the virtual environment:

On Windows:
```bash myenv\Scripts\activate
```

On macOS and Linux:
```bash
source myenv/bin/activate
```

Now that you have a virtual environment set up, you are ready to install the required libraries. ## Installing Required Libraries

You can use Python's package manager, `pip`, to install the libraries needed. Here's how to install each of the libraries discussed earlier.

1. Installing Pandas

Pandas is a fundamental library for data analysis in Python. Install it using the following command:
```bash
pip install pandas
```

2. Installing OpenPyXL

To work with Excel files that are in the .xlsx format, OpenPyXL is a great choice. Install it with:

```bash
pip install openpyxl
```

3. Installing XlsxWriter

If you are looking to create new Excel files from scratch or manipulate existing ones with advanced features, XlsxWriter is ideal. Install it using:

```bash
pip install XlsxWriter
```

4. Installing PyWin32 (Windows Only)

If you require automation with the Excel application itself (e.g., opening Excel, modifying files, etc.), you'll need PyWin32. Install it using:

```bash
pip install pywin32
```

5. Verifying Installation

After installing the libraries, it is a good practice to verify that they were installed correctly. You can do this by attempting to import them in a Python environment (e.g., a Python shell or Jupyter Notebook):

```python
```

import pandas as pd import openpyxl import xlsxwriter

import win32com.client # Only if you're using PyWin32

```
```

If no errors are thrown upon running the imports, you have successfully installed the libraries. ## Troubleshooting Installation Issues

In the event you encounter issues during installation, consider the following troubleshooting steps:

Check your internet connection: Ensure you have a stable connection as `pip` requires internet access to download packages.

Update `pip`: Sometimes an outdated version of `pip` may cause issues. Update it using:

```bash
pip install --upgrade pip
```

Check for compatibility: Ensure that the libraries you are trying to install are compatible with your version of Python.

Consult Documentation: Each library has comprehensive documentation that can provide insights into resolving common issues.

In this chapter, you have learned how to install the essential Python libraries for interacting with Excel files. The ability to read, write, and manipulate Excel data using Python opens up a world of possibilities for automation and data analysis. Now that you have these tools at your disposal, you can significantly enhance your efficiency in managing data workflows and leverage the power of Python for your Excel tasks. The next chapters will delve deeper into practical applications and coding examples, where you will see these libraries in action.

Configuring Your Excel Environment

However, to harness its full potential, it's essential to configure your Excel environment to meet your specific needs and enhance your productivity. This chapter will guide you through the various aspects of configuring your Excel setup, including customizing the ribbon, adjusting settings for optimal performance, and organizing your workspace.

1. Getting Started

Before diving into the customization options, it's important to understand the default layout of Excel. The interface consists of the Ribbon at the top, the Worksheet area where you'll input data, the Formula Bar for editing and entering formulas, and various toolbars and menus around the workspace. Familiarizing yourself with the default layout helps you identify the areas that need adjustment to fit your workflow.

2. Customizing the Ribbon

The Ribbon is designed to provide easy access to all of Excel's tools, but it can be overwhelming with its numerous tabs and groups. Customizing the Ribbon can help streamline your workflow:

2.1. Adding or Removing Tabs

Right-click on the Ribbon and select "Customize the Ribbon."

In the dialog that appears, you can see a list of tabs and groups. Check or uncheck the boxes next to the tabs you want to add or remove.

To create a new tab, click on "New Tab," then use the

commands pane to add commands to this new tab. ### 2.2. Reorganizing Ribbon Items

You can drag and drop items within the Ribbon, allowing you to position frequently used commands to a more convenient location.

Consider organizing commands logically based on your most common tasks, creating groups within your custom tabs as needed.

3. Adjusting Excel Options

Excel's settings can significantly impact your user experience. Access these options via **File > Options**. Here are a few key areas to customize:

3.1. General Settings

Default File Location: Set a specific folder for saving and opening files readily.

User Name and Initials: Update your name and initials, which appear on comments and tracked changes.

3.2. Formulas

Calculation Options: Choose between automatic or manual calculation modes. If you're working with large datasets, manual calculation can improve performance.

Error Checking: Enable or disable Excel's automatic error checking based on your preferences. ### 3.3. Advanced Options

Display Options: Adjust settings to show or hide gridlines, headings, and formula bars.

Cut, Copy, and Paste options: Modify settings to control how pasted data behaves to minimize formatting issues.

4. Setting Up Your Workspace

An organized workspace enhances focus and efficiency. Consider these steps to create a productive environment:

4.1. Using Multiple Workbooks

Keep related workbooks open side by side for easy data cross-referencing. You can arrange windows by selecting **View > Arrange All** and choosing your preferred layout.

4.2. Customizing the Quick Access Toolbar (QAT)

The QAT, located above or below the Ribbon, allows one-click access to frequently used commands:

Click the downward arrow on the QAT to customize it.

Add commands by selecting them from the list or using "More Commands" to find specific features. ### 4.3. Themes and Colors

Consider adjusting the Excel theme to improve visibility and reduce eye strain:

Go to **File > Options > General**.

Under "Personalize your copy of Microsoft Office," choose a theme that suits your visual preference. ## 5. Accessibility Features

Excel offers a range of features to enhance accessibility.

Explore options in **File > Options > Ease of Access** to adjust settings for better visibility, keyboard access, and screen reader compatibility.

6. Learning Shortcuts

Familiarize yourself with keyboard shortcuts to speed up your workflow. Customizing shortcuts and memorizing key combinations can save time on repetitive tasks. For example, learning shortcuts for common functions like Ctrl + C (Copy) and Ctrl + V (Paste) is essential.

7. Final Thoughts

Configuring your Excel environment to fit your individual needs can drastically improve your efficiency and effectiveness while working with data. By customizing the Ribbon, adjusting your options, setting up your workspace, and leveraging accessibility features, you can create a personalized setup that enhances your productivity.

Remember that every user's needs are different, and ongoing adjustments may be necessary as you learn more about Excel's features and discover new workflow patterns. Take the time to review your setup regularly and adjust it to optimize your Excel experience continually.

Dive into the next chapter as we explore advanced Excel functions and formulas that can transform your data analysis capabilities!

Chapter 2: Introduction to External Data Sources

As organizations strive to enhance their competitiveness and innovate, they often find that internal data alone is insufficient. This chapter explores the notion of external data sources, their significance, types, and the best practices for utilizing them to drive insights.

2.1 Understanding External Data Sources

External data sources refer to any data that originates outside of an organization's internal systems. Unlike internal data, which is generated from direct operations, such as sales data, customer interactions, and inventory levels, external data encompasses a diverse range of information that can provide valuable context, benchmarks, and trends. These sources can inform strategy, drive decision-making, and improve service delivery.

2.1.1 Importance of External Data

The reliance on external data stems from several crucial benefits:

Comprehensive Market Insights: External data allows organizations to gain a broader understanding of market conditions, competitor behavior, and consumer preferences. By analyzing trends in the industry or shifts in public sentiment, businesses can adapt their strategies to better align with current demands.

Enhanced Decision-Making: Access to external data sources enriches the decision-making process. When organizations incorporate external data into their analyses, they base their strategies on a more holistic view of the business landscape.

Risk Mitigation: By understanding external factors such as economic indicators, regulatory changes, and supply chain dynamics, organizations can better anticipate risks and devise strategies to mitigate them.

Innovation: External data fosters innovation by providing insights into emerging trends and technologies. Organizations can harness this information to create new products or improve existing services.

2.2 Types of External Data Sources

External data can be classified into several categories, each of which provides unique insights and data points. The following describes some common types of external data sources:

2.2.1 Public Data

Public data is information that is freely available from government entities and institutions. This includes demographic data, economic reports, census data, environmental statistics, and much more. Governments typically publish this information to foster transparency and support public research.

2.2.2 Commercial Data

Commercial data is collected and sold by third-party organizations. This data often includes consumer behavior insights, market research reports, and industry benchmarks. Companies such as Nielsen and Gartner specialize in gathering and analyzing this type of data, which can be invaluable for understanding consumer behavior and market trends.

2.2.3 Social Media Data

In today's digital age, social media platforms generate vast amounts of user-generated content. Analyzing social media data can provide insights into consumer sentiment, brand perception, and trend identification. Tools that track hashtags, mentions, and post engagements can help organizations tap into public opinion and emerging trends.

2.2.4 Academic and Research Publications

Research papers, journal articles, and academic studies offer valuable insights for organizations seeking to understand complex issues or novel methodologies. Academic institutions often publish findings that can inform best practices across various fields.

2.2.5 IoT and Sensor Data

The Internet of Things (IoT) has introduced a new dimension to data collection. Devices equipped with sensors can provide real-time data related to temperature, humidity, location, and more. This information can be harnessed for applications in smart cities, supply chain management, and predictive maintenance.

2.2.6 Market Data Feeds

Market data providers supply real-time data for financial markets, commodities, and currency exchange. This data is critical for organizations that operate in trading, investing, or any market-sensitive environment where timely information can lead to competitive advantages.

2.3 Best Practices for Utilizing External Data Sources

Leveraging external data sources effectively requires a

strategic approach. Here are some best practices to consider:

2.3.1 Data Quality Assessment

Before integrating external data into decision-making processes, organizations need to evaluate its quality. This includes assessing the credibility of the source, the accuracy of the data, its timeliness, and its relevance to the organization's specific needs.

2.3.2 Integration with Internal Data

Combining external and internal data can lead to richer insights. Organizations should establish methodologies for data integration, ensuring that insights gained from external sources complement internal data.

2.3.3 Data Governance

Establishing robust data governance frameworks is vital for managing external data usage. Organizations should create protocols for data collection, storage, sharing, and security to comply with regulations and ensure ethical practices.

2.3.4 Continuous Monitoring and Evaluation

The landscape of external data is constantly evolving. Organizations must stay abreast of changes in external data sources, evaluating their relevance and value regularly to adapt to new opportunities and challenges.

The integration of external data sources into an organization's data strategy is no longer optional; it is essential for success in a dynamic and competitive environment. By understanding the types of external data available and adopting best practices for utilization, organizations can unlock new avenues for insights that drive innovation and business growth. In the following chapters, we will delve deeper into specific external data sources, exploring how to access, analyze, and leverage this information for meaningful outcomes.

Types of External Data Sources for Python Excel

Excel Users can harness the power of Python and its libraries like `pandas`, `openpyxl`, and `xlsxwriter` to streamline their workflows, enhance their data processing capabilities, and facilitate better decision-making. In this chapter, we will explore various external data sources that can be integrated into Python Excel workflows, enhancing your data analysis and reporting capabilities.

1. Databases

1.1 Relational Databases

Relational databases are structured collections of data that can be accessed and manipulated using SQL (Structured Query Language). Common relational databases include MySQL, PostgreSQL, SQLite, and Microsoft SQL Server. Python's libraries such as `SQLAlchemy`, `sqlite3`, and `pyodbc` allow users to connect, query, and retrieve data from these databases, which can then be exported to Excel files.

Example:

```python
import pandas as pd

from sqlalchemy import create_engine

# Create a connection to a PostgreSQL database

engine = create_engine('postgresql://username:password@localhost/dbname')

# Query the database

data = pd.read_sql('SELECT * FROM your_table', engine)
```

```
# Export the data to Excel data.to_excel('output.xlsx',
index=False)
```

1.2 NoSQL Databases

NoSQL databases, such as MongoDB, Cassandra, and Redis, are designed to store unstructured or semi-structured data. Python libraries like `pymongo` for MongoDB allow users to connect and manipulate these databases efficiently. You can retrieve the necessary data and then format it into a structured form suitable for Excel.

Example:

```python
from pymongo import MongoClient import pandas as pd

# Connect to MongoDB

client = MongoClient('mongodb://localhost:27017/') db = client['your_database']

collection = db['your_collection']

# Retrieve data

data = pd.DataFrame(list(collection.find()))

# Export to Excel data.to_excel('output.xlsx',
index=False)
```


2. APIs (Application Programming Interfaces)

APIs provide a powerful means of accessing and

integrating data from various external platforms, services, and applications. Libraries such as `requests` and `http.client` in Python make it easy to consume RESTful APIs, allowing users to retrieve JSON or XML data, which can then be transformed into Excel format.

Example:

```python
import requests
import pandas as pd
# Get data from a public API
response = requests.get('https://api.example.com/data')
data = response.json()
# Convert JSON data to a DataFrame df = pd.DataFrame(data)
# Export to Excel df.to_excel('output.xlsx', index=False)
```

3. CSV and Text Files

Comma-Separated Values (CSV) and other text files remain a prevalent means of transporting data. Python's built-in `csv` module and `pandas` library make it easy to read from text files, process the data, and write it to Excel files.

Example:

```python
import pandas as pd
# Read a CSV file
data = pd.read_csv('data.csv')
```

```
# Export to Excel data.to_excel('output.xlsx',
index=False)
```

4. Web Scraping

Web scraping is the process of extracting data from websites. Libraries such as `BeautifulSoup`, `requests`, and `Scrapy` empower data analysts to gather real-time data from the web. This data can then be processed and exported to Excel for further analysis or reporting.

Example:

```python
import requests
from bs4 import BeautifulSoup import pandas as pd

# Scrape data from a website url = 'https://example.com/data' response = requests.get(url)
```

```
soup = BeautifulSoup(response.text, 'html.parser')
# Extract data data = []
for row in soup.find_all('tr'):
cols = row.find_all('td') data.append([col.text for col in cols])
# Create DataFrame and export to Excel
df = pd.DataFrame(data, columns=['Column1', 'Column2']) df.to_excel('output.xlsx', index=False)
```

5. Cloud Storage Services

With the rise of cloud computing, services like Google Drive, Dropbox, and AWS S3 enable users to access data files remotely. Libraries such as `gspread` for Google Sheets and `boto3` for AWS allow for effortless interaction with cloud-stored Excel files, enabling upload, download, and transformation of data.

Example with Google Sheets:

```python
import gspread
from oauth2client.service_account import ServiceAccountCredentials import pandas as pd
# Setup the credentials and client
scope = ["https://spreadsheets.google.com/feeds", "https://www.googleapis.com/auth/drive"] creds = ServiceAccountCredentials.from_json_keyfile_name('credentials.json', scope)
client = gspread.authorize(creds)
```

```
# Open Google Sheet and create DataFrame sheet =
client.open('your_sheet_name').sheet1       data      =
pd.DataFrame(sheet.get_all_records())

# Export   to   Excel   data.to_excel('output.xlsx',
index=False)
```

The ability to utilize Python to connect with these diverse
data sources helps create a more versatile and powerful
data analysis environment, significantly improving
decision-making processes and data-driven insights. In
the next chapter, we will look into the techniques of data
cleaning and transformation within Python, preparing it
for thorough analysis and visualization in Excel.

Common Data Formats and Protocols in Python Excel

This chapter discusses the common data formats and
protocols used in Python to work with Excel files. We will
explore various libraries and methodologies that facilitate
seamless interactions between Python and Excel, enabling
data scientists, analysts, and developers to handle data
efficiently.

1. Excel File Formats

Excel files can be saved in several formats, two of which
are predominantly used in Python for data analysis: ###
1.1. XLSX

The XLSX format is the default file format for modern
versions of Excel (Excel 2007 and later). It is based on the
Open XML format, which means it is essentially an
archive of XML files. This file format allows for large

datasets and rich formatting options. Python libraries commonly utilized to read and write this format include:

Pandas: The Pandas library has built-in support for reading and writing XLSX files using the

`read_excel()` and `to_excel()` functions, respectively. It is straightforward to use and integrates well with DataFrame operations.

OpenPyXL: This library allows for more advanced operations like modifying existing worksheets, creating charts, and more complex data manipulations within the XLSX files.

XlsxWriter: This is mainly focused on writing data to XLSX files. It provides extensive formatting options and is suitable for creating complex Excel files.

1.2. XLS

The XLS format is an older binary format used by Excel before the introduction of the XLSX format. While it may not support some modern features, it is still relevant in certain legacy systems. The libraries capable of handling XLS files include:

xlrd: This library was primarily used to read data from XLS files. However, as of version 2.0, it has removed support for XLSX. It is useful when dealing with legacy XLS files.

Pandas: Although primarily associated with XLSX, Pandas can also read XLS files through the

`read_excel()` function.

2. Data Representation in Python

In Python, data is typically represented in structures that facilitate easy manipulation. The following data formats are commonly used when working with Excel data:

2.1. DataFrames

Pandas DataFrames are the most common data format used for handling tabular data. When you read an Excel file into Python using Pandas, the data is transformed into a DataFrame, where:

Rows represent observations or individual records.

Columns represent variables or features.

This format allows for straightforward data slicing, aggregation, and transformation, making it highly efficient for data analysis.

2.2. Dictionaries

Python dictionaries can also represent data read from Excel files, especially when employing libraries like OpenPyXL or when constructing data for export. Each key-value pair represents a column and its respective data points. However, this format is less common for data manipulation when performing complex analyses, as it lacks the inherent structure of a DataFrame.

2.3. Lists and Tuples

For smaller datasets or when dealing with simple structures, lists or tuples can be used to hold rows or columns. However, this approach is limited in functionality compared to DataFrames, especially for larger datasets where operations like merging, grouping, and filtering are crucial.

3. Common Protocols for Data Exchange

When working with Excel files, certain protocols facilitate data interchange between different systems and applications.

3.1. ODBC (Open Database Connectivity)

ODBC is a standard protocol that allows applications to connect to databases, including Excel, in a uniform manner. It enables Python applications to interact with Excel files acting as databases. Libraries like `pyodbc` can be used for querying and manipulating Excel data using SQL syntax. ### 3.2. RESTful APIs

With the rise of web applications, RESTful APIs have become prevalent for data exchange. Excel files can be uploaded to cloud services that offer REST APIs (like Google Sheets). Python's mechanisms for making HTTP requests, such as the `requests` library, can be used to send and retrieve data from these API endpoints.

3.3. CSV (Comma-Separated Values)

CSV is another widely used format for data interchange, often used as a step in the process of moving data into or out of Excel. CSV files can be easily read by Pandas using `read_csv()` and can be exported using `to_csv()`. While not an Excel format per se, CSV serves as a bridge when sharing data between applications.

4. Integrating Python with Excel ### 4.1. Automating Excel Tasks

Using libraries like `openpyxl` or `pywin32`, Python can automate tasks in Excel, such as creating reports, updating datasets, or generating charts. This integration allows for greater productivity and accuracy, eliminating the need for repetitive manual work.

4.2. Data Visualization

Python's rich ecosystem of visualization libraries can be used to generate graphs and charts, which can then be exported to Excel. Libraries such as Matplotlib or Seaborn can produce high-quality visualizations, which can be inserted into the Excel sheets using `openpyxl` or exported as images.

4.3. Data Analysis

Leveraging libraries like Pandas for data analysis in conjunction with Excel allows for comprehensive data workflows. Python can perform complex analyses that can then export cleaned or transformed data back to Excel for reporting or further manipulation by users.

By understanding the common data formats and integration techniques discussed in this chapter, analysts and developers can harness the full potential of Python to enhance their productivity and streamline their workflows. As data continues to grow in importance, proficiency in these tools will be invaluable for anyone working with Excel-based data in Python.

Chapter 3: Connecting Python to APIs

In this chapter, we will explore how to connect Python to Excel for data manipulation, retrieve information from various APIs, and ultimately make this data accessible within Excel. This workflow not only enhances productivity but also allows for dynamic data analysis which is crucial in today's data-driven world.

3.1 Understanding APIs

Before diving into connections and code, it's essential to grasp what an API is. An API is a set of rules that allows different software components to communicate with each other. In data analytics, APIs are often used to retrieve data from web services, databases, and other platforms. They typically return data in formats such as JSON (JavaScript Object Notation) or XML (eXtensible Markup Language), which can then be parsed and utilized in Python.

Common use cases for APIs include:

Fetching real-time data (e.g., stock prices, weather information).

Accessing large datasets from cloud services (e.g., Google Cloud, AWS).

Integrating with social media platforms. ## 3.2 Setting Up the Environment

To work with APIs and Excel using Python, you'll need a few libraries. Ensure that you have the following

packages installed:

```bash
pip install requests pandas openpyxl
```

Requests: This library simplifies making HTTP requests to APIs.

Pandas: This powerful data manipulation library will help us structure and manage data easily.

Openpyxl: This package enables writing to Excel files. Once installed, you can start coding!

3.3 Fetching Data from an API

Let's consider a practical example. We'll use a public weather API to fetch the current weather data for a specified city. For this exercise, we'll use the OpenWeatherMap API, which requires free registration to obtain an API key.

Step 1: Get Your API Key

Sign up at [OpenWeatherMap](https://openweathermap.org).

After logging in, navigate to the API keys section, where you can generate your API key. ### Step 2: Write the Python Script

Below is a Python script that retrieves weather data and stores it in a DataFrame, which will later be saved to Excel.

```python
import requests

import pandas as pd



# Replace 'YOUR_API_KEY' with your actual OpenWeatherMap API key. API_KEY = 'YOUR_API_KEY'

CITY = 'London'

URL = f'http://api.openweathermap.org/data/2.5/weather?q={CITY}&appid={API_KEY}'

# Fetching the data
```

```python
response = requests.get(URL) data = response.json()
# Extracting relevant information weather_data = {
'City': data['name'],
'Temperature (K)': data['main']['temp'],
'Humidity (%)': data['main']['humidity'],
'Weather': data['weather'][0]['description']
}
# Creating a DataFrame
df = pd.DataFrame([weather_data])
print(df)
```

In this script:

We construct the request URL using the city name and API key.

We fetch the data using the `requests` library and parse it as JSON.

We extract relevant weather information and store it in a Pandas DataFrame. ## 3.4 Saving Data to Excel

Once we have our data in a DataFrame, it's straightforward to save this to an Excel file:

```python
# Save the DataFrame to an Excel file excel_file_path =
'weather_data.xlsx'          df.to_excel(excel_file_path,
index=False)
```

print(f'Data saved to {excel_file_path}')

```
```

This simple line of code saves our DataFrame to an Excel file named `weather_data.xlsx`. The `index=False` parameter ensures that we do not write row indices to the Excel file.

3.5 Automating Data Updates

One of the main advantages of connecting Python, Excel, and APIs is the ability to automate data retrieval. This means you can set the script to run periodically or on-demand to update the data within your Excel file.

Using a task scheduler like Windows Task Scheduler or cron jobs on Unix-based systems can facilitate this automation. Simply set the script to execute at desired intervals, ensuring you always have the latest data without manual intervention.

Integrating Python with Excel and APIs opens up a wide range of possibilities for data analysis and reporting. In this chapter, we have explored how to connect to APIs, retrieve data, and seamlessly integrate it into Excel using Python. This method not only streamlines workflows but also enhances the accuracy and timeliness of the information at your disposal.

Understanding API Basics and Authentication

They serve as bridges that allow developers to integrate external functionalities and data into their own applications, enabling a range of possibilities from simple data retrieval to complex business processes. This chapter aims to provide a foundational understanding of APIs, their purpose, and the fundamentals of authentication, ensuring that readers are equipped to use and implement APIs effectively.

1.1 What is an API?

An API is a set of rules and protocols that allows different software programs to communicate. It specifies how software components should interact, whether they reside on the same machine or are distributed across different servers. APIs are present in various forms:

Web APIs enable communication over the internet using the HTTP protocol.

Library APIs provide sets of functions for programming languages to extend their capabilities.

Operating System APIs facilitate interaction between applications and the underlying OS.

APIs simplify the development process by allowing developers to build on top of pre-existing functionalities rather than reinventing the wheel. For instance, instead of building a payment processing system from scratch, a developer can use APIs from payment platforms like PayPal or Stripe.

1.1.1 RESTful APIs

One of the most common types of APIs used today is the RESTful API (Representational State Transfer). RESTful APIs utilize standard HTTP methods such as GET, POST, PUT, and DELETE to perform operations:

GET: Retrieve data from the server.

POST: Send data to the server to create a new resource.

PUT: Update an existing resource on the server.

DELETE: Remove a resource from the server.

RESTful APIs thrive on statelessness, meaning each request from a client to server must contain all the information needed to understand and process the request, making them scalable and efficient.

1.2 The Importance of API Authentication

While APIs provide a powerful mechanism for web applications to interact, they also expose sensitive data and functionalities. As such, implementing proper authentication is critical to ensure that only authorized users can access specific APIs. API authentication verifies user identity before granting access to resources, protecting the integrity and confidentiality of data.

1.2.1 Common Authentication Mechanisms

There are several methods for API authentication, each offering varying levels of security and complexity:

API Keys:

An API key is a unique identifier generated by the server for each user or application. It is sent along with API requests to authenticate the client.

While easy to implement, API keys can become vulnerable if not handled securely (e.g., embedding keys in client-side code).

Basic Authentication:

This method involves sending a username and password encoded in Base64 with each request.

Basic Authentication is straightforward but should always be used in conjunction with HTTPS to avoid exposing credentials.

OAuth 2.0:

OAuth 2.0 is a more complex and secure framework that allows third-party applications to access user data without sharing passwords. It works with access tokens, which are granted after users authenticate themselves using their credentials on a related authentication server.

OAuth is widely used by major platforms—like Google and Facebook—for authorizing APIs.

JWT (JSON Web Tokens):

JWT is a compact, URL-safe means of representing claims to be transferred between two parties. It can carry additional metadata and is often used for authorization in RESTful APIs.

Once the user is authenticated, a JWT is generated and returned, which is then passed in subsequent requests.

1.2.2 Best Practices for API Security

To enhance the security of API authentication, developers should consider the following best practices:

Use HTTPS: Always utilize HTTPS for encrypted requests, preventing man-in-the-middle (MITM) attacks.

Implement Rate Limiting: Limit the number of requests a user can make within a certain time frame to deter abuse and potential denial-of-service attacks.

Validate Input: Ensure that input from users is validated to protect against injection attacks.

Regularly Rotate Keys and Secrets: Change API keys and secrets periodically to minimizes the risk of them being compromised.

Monitor and Log Access: Keep track of API access patterns to spot suspicious or unauthorized activities.

As the digital world continues to evolve, understanding API basics and authentication is fundamental for developers and organizations seeking to leverage external services and enhance their applications. By familiarizing oneself with different types of APIs and authentication methods, developers can secure their applications, maintain user trust, and contribute to the vibrant ecosystem of interconnected services.

Fetching and Parsing Data from APIs

This chapter will guide you through the process of fetching and parsing data from APIs, presenting best practices, tools, and examples to equip you with the skills you need to interact effectively with APIs.

Understanding APIs

Before delving into the technical details, it's essential to grasp the concept of APIs. An API is a set of rules and protocols that allows different software applications to communicate with one another. It defines the methods and data formats that applications can use to request and exchange information. APIs can be public, private, or partner-specific, and they often expose RESTful endpoints or SOAP services for data exchange.

Types of APIs

REST APIs: Representational State Transfer (REST) APIs are based on standard HTTP methods such as GET, POST, PUT, and DELETE. They communicate using data formats like JSON or XML, making them lightweight and easy to use.

SOAP APIs: Simple Object Access Protocol (SOAP) APIs use XML-based messaging and are more rigid in structure. SOAP is often considered more secure but can be more complex to work with compared to REST APIs.

GraphQL: An alternative to REST, GraphQL allows clients to request only the data they need. It provides a more flexible approach for querying data but requires some familiarity with its syntax.

Fetching Data from APIs

Fetching data from APIs can typically be approached in the same way, regardless of the specific type. The process involves sending a request to the API endpoint and receiving a response. Below, we'll discuss how to fetch data from a RESTful API using popular programming languages, including Python and JavaScript.

Fetching Data Using JavaScript

JavaScript is well-suited for client-side API requests. The `fetch` API simplifies the process of making network requests:

```javascript
async function fetchData(url) { try {

const response = await fetch(url); if (!response.ok) {

throw new Error(`HTTP error! status:
${response.status}`);
```

```
  }
  const data = await response.json(); console.log(data);
  } catch (error) {
  console.error('Fetch error:', error);
  }
}

const apiUrl = 'https://api.example.com/data';
fetchData(apiUrl);
```

In this example, an asynchronous function `fetchData` is defined to call the API. It checks if the response is successful and then parses the JSON data.

Fetching Data Using Python

Python offers several libraries, such as `requests`, that facilitate API interactions. Below is an example of how to fetch data using this library:

```python
import requests

def fetch_data(url):
    try:
        response = requests.get(url)
        response.raise_for_status()  # Raises an error for bad responses
        data = response.json() # Parse JSON response
        print(data)
    except requests.exceptions.RequestException as e:
        print(f'Error occurred: {e}')
```

```
api_url        =        'https://api.example.com/data'
fetch_data(api_url)
```

Here, the `fetch_data` function uses the `requests` library to send a GET request, handling any potential errors and parsing the returned JSON response.

Parsing JSON Data

Once you have fetched the data, the next step is parsing it. JSON (JavaScript Object Notation) is the most common format being returned when calling APIs due to its simplicity and ease of use.

Navigating JSON Data

JSON data is organized as key-value pairs. Here's a simple example of a JSON response:

```json
{
"user": {
"id": 1,
"name": "John Doe",
"email": "john.doe@example.com"
},
"posts": [
{
"id": 101,
"title": "Hello World",
```

```
    "content": "This is my first post!"
  },
  {

    "id": 102,
    "title": "API Basics",
    "content": "Learning how to work with APIs."
  }
 ]
}
```

To parse this data in JavaScript, you can access it using dot notation or bracket notation:

```javascript
console.log(data.user.name);    //    "John    Doe"
console.log(data.posts[0].title); // "Hello World"
```

In Python, you can access the elements of the JSON response similarly:

```python
print(data['user']['name']) # "John Doe"
print(data['posts'][0]['title']) # "Hello World"
```

Handling Nested Data

APIs often return nested data structures. Navigating these requires understanding the shape of the data returned. Using loops and conditionals can help traverse these structures effectively.

```python
for post in data['posts']:

print(f"Post Title: {post['title']}")
```

Error Handling

When working with APIs, it's crucial to implement error handling. Common issues include connection errors, timeout errors, and non-success status codes. Robust error handling ensures that your application can gracefully recover from issues. Each programming language has its idiomatic way of handling exceptions, as demonstrated in previous examples.

Rate Limiting and Throttling

APIs often have rate limits to prevent abuse of their services. It's important to read the API documentation to understand these limits and handle retries or exponential backoff strategies in case you exceed them.

Fetching and parsing data from APIs is a foundational skill for modern developers. With the knowledge gained in this chapter, you should be well-equipped to interact with various APIs, construct requests, and handle responses effectively. Moreover, understanding error handling, data formats, and the structure of JSON will enable you to build more reliable and user-friendly applications.

Chapter 4: Integrating Python with SQL Databases

This chapter will explore how to use Python as a bridge between Excel and SQL, leveraging the strengths of both to create comprehensive data solutions.

4.1 Overview of Data Integration

Data integration is the process of combining data from different sources into a unified view, enabling organizations to gain insights from disparate datasets. Excel remains a popular tool for data management, often serving as a user-friendly interface for data analysis. On the other hand, SQL databases provide robust storage, querying capabilities, and efficient handling of large datasets.

This integration allows users to perform the following tasks:

Import data from Excel into SQL databases for long-term storage and complex querying.

Export query results from SQL databases into Excel for analysis and reporting.

Automate workflows to streamline the process of data transfer. ## 4.2 Setting Up the Environment

To integrate Python with Excel and SQL databases, you'll need to set up your environment by installing the necessary libraries. The most commonly used libraries for this purpose are:

pandas: A powerful data manipulation library that can read and write Excel files and interface with SQL databases.

openpyxl or **xlrd**: Libraries for reading and writing Excel files.

SQLAlchemy: A popular SQL toolkit and Object Relational Mapping (ORM) system that facilitates interaction with SQL databases.

pyodbc or **sqlite3**: Libraries that allow Python to connect to various databases. You can install these libraries using pip:

```bash
pip install pandas openpyxl sqlalchemy pyodbc
```

4.3 Importing Excel Data into SQL Databases ### 4.3.1 Reading Data from Excel

Using Python's pandas library, you can easily read data from Excel files. The following example demonstrates how to read data from an Excel file named `data.xlsx`.

```python
import pandas as pd
# Load the Excel file excel_file = 'data.xlsx'
# Read the data into a DataFrame
data = pd.read_excel(excel_file, sheet_name='Sheet1')
```

In this example, `pd.read_excel` is used to load data from the specified sheet of the Excel file into a DataFrame called `data`.

4.3.2 Connecting to a SQL Database

Once the data is loaded into a DataFrame, the next step is to connect to a SQL database. Here, we will use SQLAlchemy to facilitate this connection:

```python
from sqlalchemy import create_engine

# Create a SQLAlchemy engine

engine = create_engine('sqlite:///my_database.db')  # Example for SQLite
```

With the engine created, you can now easily write the DataFrame to the SQL database. ### 4.3.3 Writing Data to SQL

To export the DataFrame to a SQL table, use the `to_sql` method from pandas:

```python
# Write the DataFrame to a SQL table named 'my_table'
data.to_sql('my_table', con=engine, if_exists='replace', index=False)
```

The `if_exists='replace'` argument tells pandas to replace the existing table with the new data if it already exists. This method can also append data if needed by changing the parameter to `'append'`.

4.4 Exporting SQL Data to Excel ### 4.4.1 Querying Data from SQL

To export data from a SQL database back to Excel, you'll first want to run a SQL query to retrieve the desired data:

```python
query = 'SELECT * FROM my_table'

result = pd.read_sql_query(query, con=engine)
```

The `pd.read_sql_query` function executes the SQL query and returns the results as a DataFrame. ### 4.4.2 Writing Data to Excel

Once you have the query results in a DataFrame, you can easily export it back to Excel:

```python
output_file = 'output_data.xlsx'

result.to_excel(output_file,                 index=False, sheet_name='Results')
```

This code will create an Excel file named `output_data.xlsx`, containing the results of the SQL query in a sheet titled 'Results'.

4.5 Automating the Process

One of the significant advantages of using Python for this integration is automation. By scheduling Python scripts using tools like cron (on Unix systems) or Windows Task Scheduler, you can automate the flow of data between Excel and SQL databases.

An example script might include reading from Excel, processing the data, writing to SQL, running analyses, and exporting results back to Excel, all executed seamlessly on a predefined schedule.

Integrating Python Excel with SQL databases opens up a world of possibilities for efficient data management and analysis. With the capabilities provided by libraries like pandas and SQLAlchemy, users can easily move data between Excel and SQL, automate workflows, and gain valuable insights from their data. As we move forward, mastering these integration techniques will empower organizations to make data-driven decisions with greater speed and accuracy.

Connecting to SQL Databases Using Python

Python, a versatile and powerful programming language, provides several libraries and frameworks that make connecting to and managing SQL databases remarkably straightforward. This chapter explores the various methods for connecting to SQL databases using Python, with a focus on popular libraries such as SQLite, MySQL, and PostgreSQL.

Understanding SQL Databases

SQL (Structured Query Language) is a standardized language for managing and manipulating relational databases. It allows users to create, read, update, and delete data stored in tables. Common types of SQL databases include:

SQLite: A lightweight, serverless database ideal for smaller applications and embedded systems.

MySQL: An open-source relational database management system used widely in web applications.

PostgreSQL: An advanced open-source database known for its robustness and support for complex queries.

Setting Up the Environment

Before diving into connecting Python with SQL databases, you will need to have Python installed on your machine along with the required libraries corresponding to the database you intend to use.

To manage libraries in Python, we typically use `pip`, the package installer. Here's how to install some popular libraries:

```bash
# For SQLite (comes pre-installed with Python)

# You do not need to install this; it is part of the standard library.

# For MySQL

pip install mysql-connector-python

# For PostgreSQL pip install psycopg2
```

Connecting to SQLite Database

SQLite is great for applications with a small footprint since it operates directly on the database file. Here's how you can connect to an SQLite database:

```python
import sqlite3
```

Connect to the SQLite database (it will create the database file if it doesn't exist) connection = sqlite3.connect('example.db')

Create a cursor object using the connection cursor = connection.cursor()

Create a table

cursor.execute('CREATE TABLE IF NOT EXISTS users (id INTEGER PRIMARY KEY, name TEXT, age INTEGER)')

Insert a record

cursor.execute('INSERT INTO users (name, age) VALUES (?, ?)', ('Alice', 30))

Commit the changes and close the connection connection.commit()

connection.close()
```
```

Connecting to MySQL Database

For MySQL, you need to ensure that the MySQL server is running. Once installed, you can connect using the MySQL connector as shown below.

```python
import mysql.connector
```

```python
# Establish the connection to the database try:

connection = mysql.connector.connect( host='localhost', user='your_username', password='your_password',

database='your_database'  # Optional, can be specified later
)

# Create a cursor object cursor = connection.cursor()

# Create a table

cursor.execute('CREATE TABLE IF NOT EXISTS products (product_id INT AUTO_INCREMENT PRIMARY KEY, name VARCHAR(255), price DECIMAL(10,2))')

# Insert a record

cursor.execute('INSERT INTO products (name, price) VALUES (%s, %s)', ('Widget', 19.99))

# Commit the transaction connection.commit()

except mysql.connector.Error as err: print(f"Error: {err}")

finally:

if          connection.is_connected():          cursor.close() connection.close()
```

Connecting to PostgreSQL Database

PostgreSQL, known for its performance and scalability, requires a running instance of the database. Here's how you can connect using Python:

```python
import psycopg2
```

```
# Establish a connection to the PostgreSQL database try:

connection    =    psycopg2.connect(    host='localhost',
database='your_database',              user='your_username',
password='your_password'
)

# Create a cursor object cursor = connection.cursor()

# Create a table

cursor.execute('CREATE TABLE IF NOT EXISTS orders
(order_id SERIAL PRIMARY KEY, product_id INT,
quantity INT)')

# Insert a record

cursor.execute('INSERT INTO orders (product_id,
quantity) VALUES (%s, %s)', (1, 100))

# Commit the changes connection.commit()

except psycopg2.DatabaseError as e: print(f"Error {e}")

finally:

if connection: cursor.close() connection.close()
```
```

## Handling Exceptions

When working with databases, it is essential to use exception handling to manage any potential errors gracefully. Using `try-except` blocks, as demonstrated in the previous examples, helps capture database connection errors or query execution errors.

## Querying Data

Once you have established a connection and inserted some
```

data, you can run queries to retrieve information. Here is how to do it for each of the databases:

Querying from SQLite

```python
connection = sqlite3.connect('example.db') cursor = connection.cursor() cursor.execute('SELECT * FROM users')
```

```python
rows = cursor.fetchall() for row in rows:
print(row)
connection.close()
```

Querying from MySQL
```python
connection = mysql.connector.connect( host='localhost',
user='your_username',        password='your_password',
database='your_database'
)
cursor = connection.cursor() cursor.execute('SELECT *
FROM products')
for row in cursor.fetchall(): print(row)
connection.close()
```

Querying from PostgreSQL
```python
connection   =   psycopg2.connect(   host='localhost',
database='your_database',        user='your_username',
password='your_password'
)
cursor = connection.cursor() cursor.execute('SELECT *
FROM orders')
for row in cursor.fetchall():
print(row)
```

connection.close()
```
` ` `

Connecting to SQL databases using Python is a vital skill for anyone looking to develop data-driven applications. With libraries like `sqlite3`, `mysql-connector-python`, and `psycopg2`, the process is efficient and Pythonic. Understanding how to send queries, handle connections, and manage data allows you to build flexible applications capable of robust data management.

## Executing Queries and Fetching Results in Excel with python

With Python, executing queries and fetching results can be streamlined regardless of whether your data resides in a relational database, a CSV file, or even an Excel spreadsheet. This chapter explores the process of querying data and exporting the results into Excel, leveraging Python's powerful libraries such as SQLAlchemy, Pandas, and openpyxl.

---

## 1. Setting the Stage ### 1.1 Prerequisites

Before diving into executing queries and fetching results, it is essential to ensure that your environment is set up correctly. For this chapter, you will need:

Python installed on your machine (preferably Python 3.x).

Libraries: `pandas`, `openpyxl`, `sqlalchemy`, and `sqlite3` (or any other relevant database connector based on your database).
```

An understanding of SQL queries.

You can install the required libraries via pip:

```bash
pip install pandas openpyxl sqlalchemy
```

1.2 Understanding the Data Context

Consider a scenario where you have a dataset stored in a SQLite database or an Excel file with sales data for a retail company. The example data could contain fields like `OrderID`, `Product`, `Quantity`, `Price`, and

`Date`. Your goal could be to extract insights, such as total sales for specific products or daily sales trends.

---

2. Connecting to a Database

To execute SQL queries, we first need to establish a connection to a database. Below we will illustrate how to connect to a SQLite database, but the same principles apply for other databases with minor modifications.

2.1 Establishing a Connection

```python
import sqlite3

# Establishing a connection to the SQLite database
connection = sqlite3.connect('sales_data.db')
```

In this snippet, we connect to a SQLite database called `sales_data.db`. If you were using another SQL database like MySQL or PostgreSQL, you would use SQLAlchemy:

64

```python
from sqlalchemy import create_engine

# Creating a connection to a PostgreSQL database

engine                                =
create_engine('postgresql://username:password@localhos
t:5432/sales_db')
```

---

3. Executing Queries

Once we have established a connection, we can execute SQL queries to fetch data. ### 3.1 Fetching Data from a Database

Here's how to execute a simple SQL query using Pandas, which works seamlessly with SQLAlchemy:

```python
import pandas as pd

# SQL Query to fetch total sales data

query = "SELECT Product, SUM(Price * Quantity) as Total_Sales FROM Sales GROUP BY Product;"

# Executing the query and loading data into a DataFrame
sales_data = pd.read_sql(query, engine)
```

This query will give you the total sales for each product, neatly stored in a Pandas DataFrame for easier manipulation and analysis.

3.2 Handling Errors

It's crucial to handle potential errors when executing queries. Employ try-except blocks to catch exceptions gracefully.

```python
try:
```

sales_data = pd.read_sql(query, engine) except Exception as e:

print(f"An error occurred: {e}")

```
```

---

4. Fetching Results

With the query executed and results stored in a DataFrame, the next step is to export these results to an Excel file.

4.1 Exporting Data to Excel

You can export the DataFrame to an Excel file using Pandas. Ensure you specify the filename and format:

```python
# Exporting the DataFrame to an Excel file
sales_data.to_excel('total_sales.xlsx', index=False, engine='openpyxl')
```

This creates an Excel file named `total_sales.xlsx` in the current directory with the fetched query results. ### 4.2 Customizing Excel Output

Pandas offers additional options to format your Excel

sheets. You can add more sheets, format cells, and style the output for better readability.

```python
with pd.ExcelWriter('formatted_sales_data.xlsx', engine='openpyxl') as writer: sales_data.to_excel(writer, sheet_name='Total Sales', index=False)

# Additional data

df_another = pd.DataFrame({'Category': ['A', 'B'], 'Value': [10, 20]})                df_another.to_excel(writer, sheet_name='Category Overview', index=False)
```

In this chapter, we covered the essential steps for executing queries and fetching results in Excel using Python. By leveraging libraries like Pandas and SQLAlchemy, you can efficiently manipulate and analyze data, enabling you to make data-driven decisions with ease.

5.1 Key Takeaways

Establish connection to databases using SQLAlchemy or direct connectors.

Execute SQL queries and load data into a Pandas DataFrame.

Export results easily to Excel while maintaining flexibility to format as needed.

As you progress in your data analytics journey, mastering these tasks will empower you to extract valuable insights from data more effectively and share them in a visually appealing format.

Chapter 5: Working with NoSQL Databases

In recent years, the data landscape has transformed dramatically. With the explosive growth of data generated by web applications, IoT devices, mobile apps, and social networks, traditional relational databases have shown limitations in terms of scalability, flexibility, and performance. Enter NoSQL (Not Only SQL) databases, a category of databases designed to handle large volumes of unstructured and semi- structured data with high velocity and variability.

NoSQL databases come in various flavors, including document stores, key-value stores, wide-column stores, and graph databases. Each type is tailored to specific use cases and offers unique advantages. This chapter will explore these different types and how to work effectively with NoSQL databases.

5.1 Types of NoSQL Databases ### 5.1.1 Document Stores

Document databases, like MongoDB and Couchbase, are designed to store data as documents in formats such as JSON or BSON. Each document can have a different structure, allowing for greater flexibility in data representation. This format is particularly well-suited for applications with varying data requirements, such as content management systems or e-commerce platforms.

Key Features:

Schema flexibility

Nested data structures

Powerful querying and indexing capabilities ### 5.1.2 Key-Value Stores

Key-value databases, such as Redis and Amazon DynamoDB, organize data as pairs of keys and values. This simple structure allows for efficient retrieval and storage, making key-value stores ideal for caching, session management, and real-time analytics.

Key Features:

Fast read and write operations

Scalability

High availability and fault tolerance ### 5.1.3 Wide-Column Stores

Wide-column stores, like Apache Cassandra and HBase, store data in tables with an arbitrary number of columns per row. This format can handle large datasets and is optimized for high write and read performance. They are commonly used in scenarios where data is sparse or varies significantly across rows.

Key Features:

Scalability across distributed systems

Suitable for large-scale data applications

Efficient for time-series data and analytics ### 5.1.4 Graph Databases

Graph databases, such as Neo4j and Amazon Neptune, are designed for handling interconnected data and relationships. They store data in graph structures, using nodes, edges, and properties to represent entities and their relationships. These databases are ideal for applications like social networks, recommendation systems, and fraud detection.

Key Features:

Efficient handling of connected data

Powerful relationship queries

Ability to model complex networks ## 5.2 Benefits of NoSQL Databases

Working with NoSQL databases offers several advantages:

Scalability: Many NoSQL databases are designed for horizontal scaling, allowing them to handle more data by adding more servers to the system.

Performance: NoSQL databases can provide lower latency for specific workloads, particularly for write-heavy or read-heavy operations.

Flexibility: With schema-less designs, NoSQL databases allow for rapid iteration and iteration in applications that require frequent changes to data structures.

Handling Big Data: NoSQL technologies can process large amounts of unstructured or semi- structured data, making them well-suited for big data applications.

5.3 Getting Started with NoSQL Databases ### 5.3.1

Choosing the Right NoSQL Database

When selecting a NoSQL database, consider the following factors:

Data Model: Analyze the structure of your data to determine whether document, key-value, wide- column, or graph models are more appropriate.

Use Case: Identify your application's requirements, such as scalability, read/write performance, and querying capabilities.

Community and Support: Evaluate the maturity and community support for the database, as well as the available documentation and tools.

5.3.2 Installation and Setup

The installation process varies depending on the database chosen. Most NoSQL databases provide comprehensive documentation on how to install and configure the system on your machine or cloud environment. This usually involves:

Downloading the database package.

Configuring necessary settings (e.g., storage, ports).

Starting the database service.

Using the relevant drivers or APIs to connect to your applications. ### 5.3.3 Basic Operations

After setting up your chosen NoSQL database, you'll typically perform similar operations to those common in relational databases but adapted to the NoSQL model:

CRUD Operations: Create, Read, Update, and Delete operations are fundamental. Being familiar with the syntax of the database will be essential.

Indexing: To optimize query performance, understanding how to create and manage indexes based on your queries and data access patterns is crucial.

Data Modeling: Thoughtful data modeling is essential in a NoSQL context. This includes creating the right document structure in document stores or defining the appropriate key-value pairs.

Replication and Sharding: For scalability and reliability, knowing how to configure replication (for data redundancy) and sharding (to distribute data across multiple nodes) will be advantageous.

5.4 Real-World Applications of NoSQL

NoSQL databases have been adopted across various industries for different use cases:

E-commerce: Managing product catalogs with flexible schemas and handling varying product attributes.

Social Media: Storing user profiles and connections in graph databases to optimize relationship queries.

Big Data Analytics: Collecting and analyzing large datasets generated from IoT devices.

Gaming: Storing player data, sessions, and real-time analytics.

NoSQL databases present a powerful alternative to traditional relational databases, allowing developers to create flexible, scalable, and high-performance applications. Understanding the various types of NoSQL databases, their strengths, and how to work with them is essential for leveraging modern data architectures effectively. As the data landscape continues to evolve, mastering NoSQL technologies will undoubtedly be a critical skill for developers, data engineers, and architects alike.

Connecting to NoSQL Databases (e.g., MongoDB) with Python

This is where NoSQL databases, such as MongoDB, rise to prominence. NoSQL databases provide flexible data models, horizontal scalability, and the ability to handle a diverse range of formats. In this chapter, we'll explore how to connect to a NoSQL database, specifically MongoDB, using Python, allowing you to leverage its benefits in your applications.

Why Choose MongoDB?

MongoDB is one of the most popular NoSQL databases available today. It is document-oriented and stores data in the form of JSON-like documents, making it easy to work with complex data structures. Here are some of the reasons developers choose MongoDB:

Schema Flexibility: In MongoDB, documents can have different fields and structures, allowing developers to iterate and evolve their data models without downtime.

Rich Queries: MongoDB provides a powerful query

language that supports both simple and complex queries.

Scalability: Built with scalability in mind, MongoDB can easily handle large volumes of data by sharding and replica sets.

Strong Community Support: A large developer community and extensive documentation make it easier to find resources and support.

Setting Up MongoDB

Before we can connect to MongoDB using Python, you will need to have MongoDB installed and running on your machine or accessible through a cloud service.

Installation

You can download and install MongoDB from the official website. Alternatively, you can use a cloud service like MongoDB Atlas, which provides a managed instance of MongoDB.

Local Installation:

Visit the [MongoDB Download Center](https://www.mongodb.com/try/download/community) and choose the version compatible with your operating system.

Follow the installation instructions specific to your platform.

Once installed, start the MongoDB server using the command `mongod` in your terminal.

Using MongoDB Atlas:

Go to [MongoDB Atlas](https://www.mongodb.com/cloud/atlas) and create an account.

Create a new cluster and follow the instructions to set it up.

You will be provided with a connection string to connect your application to the cloud database. ## Connecting to MongoDB with Python

To work with MongoDB in Python, we will use the `pymongo` library, which is a

powerful and user-friendly driver for interacting with MongoDB.

Installation of pymongo

To install `pymongo`, you can use pip, the Python package manager. Run the following command in your terminal:

```bash
pip install pymongo
```

Basic Connection Example

Now that you have `pymongo` installed, let's establish a connection to the MongoDB database. Below is a basic example illustrating how to connect to both a local instance and a cloud instance of MongoDB.

Connecting to a Local MongoDB Instance

```python
from pymongo import MongoClient
```

```python
# Create a MongoClient to the running MongoDB instance
client = MongoClient('localhost', 27017)
```

Access a database

```python
db = client['mydatabase']
```

Access a collection collection = db['mycollection']

```python
print("Connected to MongoDB!")
```
```

#### Connecting to MongoDB Atlas

If you're working with MongoDB Atlas, you'll use the connection string provided by Atlas:

```python
from pymongo import MongoClient

# Replace the <password> and <dbname> with your information uri =
"mongodb+srv://<username>:<password>@cluster0.mongodb.net/<dbname>?retryWrites=true&w=w=majority"
client = MongoClient(uri)
```

Access a database

```python
db = client['mydatabase']
```

Access a collection collection = db['mycollection']

```python
print("Connected to MongoDB Atlas!")
```
```

Verifying Your Connection

A simple way to ensure your connection is successful is by listing the databases available on the MongoDB server:

```python
# List all the databases

databases           =           client.list_database_names()
print("Databases available:", databases)
```

Performing CRUD Operations

Once you're connected, you can perform Create, Read, Update, and Delete (CRUD) operations on your collections.

Create

To insert a document into a collection:

```python
# Example document document = {

"name": "Alice", "age": 28,

"city": "New York"

}

# Insert the document

result           =           collection.insert_one(document)
print("Document inserted with ID:", result.inserted_id)
```

Read

To read documents from a collection:

```python
```

```python
# Find one document
person = collection.find_one({"name": "Alice"})
print("Found document:", person)
# Find all documents people = collection.find() for person in people:
print(person)
```

Update

To update an existing document:

```python
# Update a document
collection.update_one({"name": "Alice"}, {"$set": {"age": 29}})
# Verify the update
updated_person = collection.find_one({"name": "Alice"})
print("Updated document:", updated_person)
```

Delete

To delete a document:

```python
# Delete a document collection.delete_one({"name": "Alice"})
# Verify deletion
deleted_person = collection.find_one({"name": "Alice"})
```

```
print("After deletion:", deleted_person)
```
```
```

We discussed the advantages of using MongoDB, how to set it up locally or in the cloud, and performed basic CRUD operations using the `pymongo` library. With these skills, you can begin to integrate NoSQL data storage into your Python applications, paving the way for more flexible and scalable data handling in your projects. As you continue your journey, consider exploring advanced topics such as indexing, aggregation, and performance tuning to fully harness the capabilities of MongoDB in your applications.

Handling JSON Data and Queries with Python

JSON (JavaScript Object Notation) has become the de facto standard for data interchange on the web. Its lightweight nature, easy readability, and compatibility with various programming languages make it an ideal choice for representing structured data. Python, with its extensive libraries and straightforward syntax, provides comprehensive support for working with JSON data. In this chapter, we will explore how to parse, generate, and manipulate JSON data in Python, as well as how to perform queries on this data effectively.

Understanding JSON Structure

Before diving into Python's JSON handling capabilities, let's briefly discuss the structure of JSON. JSON data consists of key-value pairs and can be nested within arrays and objects. Here's a simple example of JSON data representing a collection of books:

```json
{
"books": [
{
"title": "To Kill a Mockingbird", "author": "Harper Lee",
"published": 1960
},
{
"title": "1984",
"author": "George Orwell", "published": 1949
}
]
}
```

In this structure:

The outer structure is a JSON object that contains a key `books`, which maps to an array of book objects.

Each book object contains three properties: `title`, `author`, and `published`. ## Loading JSON Data in Python

To work with JSON data in Python, we primarily use the `json` standard library, which provides methods to parse JSON strings and files.

Reading JSON from a String

To load JSON from a string, you can use the

`json.loads()` function. Here's an example:

```python
import json

json_string = '''
{
"books": [
{
"title": "To Kill a Mockingbird", "author": "Harper Lee", "published": 1960
},
{
"title": "1984",
"author": "George Orwell", "published": 1949
}
]
}
'''

data = json.loads(json_string) print(data)
```

Reading JSON from a File

For larger datasets, you might have your JSON stored in a file. You can use the `json.load()` method to read from a file:

```python
with open('books.json', 'r') as file:
```

```
data = json.load(file)
print(data)
```

Accessing and Manipulating JSON Data

Once JSON data is loaded into Python, it is typically represented as a combination of dictionaries and lists. You can access and manipulate this data using standard Python operations.

Accessing Data

To retrieve data from a JSON object, you can access it using the dictionary methods:

```python
# Accessing the list of books books = data['books']
```

```python
# Accessing the title of the first book first_book_title = books[0]['title']

print(first_book_title) # Output: To Kill a Mockingbird
```

Updating Data

You can also modify the JSON data:

```python
# Adding a new book new_book = {
"title": "The Great Gatsby", "author": "F. Scott Fitzgerald", "published": 1925
}
data['books'].append(new_book)
```

```python
print(data)
```

Deleting Data

To remove a book from the collection:

```python
# Removing the second book del data['books'][1]
print(data)
```

Writing JSON Data Back

After manipulating JSON data, you may want to save it back to a file or convert it to a string. Use the `json.dumps()` method to convert data to a JSON formatted string and the `json.dump()` method to write it to a file.

Writing JSON to a String

```python
json_output = json.dumps(data, indent=4)
print(json_output)
```

Writing JSON to a File

```python
with open('updated_books.json', 'w') as file:
json.dump(data, file, indent=4)
```

Querying JSON Data

When working with large JSON datasets, it often becomes necessary to query this data. You can build more complex logic using list comprehensions and filtering.

Simple Queries

For example, if you want to find all books published after 1950:

```python
recent_books = [book for book in data['books'] if book['published'] > 1950] print(recent_books)
```

Complex Queries

For more complex queries, you might want to use libraries like `pandas`, which allow for advanced data manipulation and querying capabilities.

```python
import pandas as pd

# Convert JSON to DataFrame

df = pd.json_normalize(data['books'])

# Query books by author

orwell_books = df[df['author'] == 'George Orwell']
print(orwell_books)
```

In this chapter, we covered the essentials of handling JSON data in Python, from loading and manipulating data to performing queries. The ability to work with JSON efficiently is invaluable, especially in web development and data analysis. By mastering these techniques, you'll be well-equipped to handle a wide range of data processing tasks. In the next chapter, we will explore advanced topics like integrating JSON APIs and asynchronous data fetching in Python.

Chapter 6: Importing and Exporting Data with CSV and Excel Files

Whether you're handling small datasets or large databases, knowing how to manipulate data using CSV (Comma-Separated Values) and Excel files can streamline your workflow and enhance collaboration. This chapter focuses on the importance of these file formats, how to effectively use them, and best practices for ensuring data integrity during the transfer process.

6.1 Understanding CSV and Excel Files ### 6.1.1 What is CSV?

CSV is a simple file format used to store tabular data, where each line of the file corresponds to a row in the table, and each value within that line is separated by a comma (or other specified delimiter). This makes CSV a straightforward and platform-independent way to exchange data. Key features of CSV files include:

Compatibility: Easily accessible by various programs, including text editors, spreadsheets, and databases.

Simplicity: The structure is uncomplicated, which means it can be manually edited if necessary.

Lightweight: CSV files are generally smaller in size compared to other formats, as they do not contain any additional formatting metadata.

6.1.2 What is Excel?

Excel is a powerful spreadsheet application developed by Microsoft, widely used for data analysis, visualization, and storage. Excel files can be saved in different formats, with the most common being `.xls` and `.xlsx`. Key features of

Excel files include:

Rich Formatting: Excel allows for extensive formatting options, including cell colors, fonts, and formulas.

Data Manipulation: Advanced tools for sorting, filtering, and calculating data, making Excel a go-to for analysts.

Charts and Graphs: Integration of visual representation tools for easier interpretation of data. ## 6.2 Why Import and Export Data?

Understanding how to import and export data between different file formats is essential for several reasons:

Data Integration: Importing enables aggregation of data from diverse sources, creating a holistic view for analysis.

Data Sharing: Exporting facilitates collaboration with team members or external stakeholders who may use different systems or tools.

Data Backup and Migration: Ensuring that data can be easily backed up or migrated from one system to another, which is crucial for data continuity and security.

6.3 Importing Data

6.3.1 Importing from CSV Files

When importing data from a CSV file, it is essential to follow a structured approach. The steps generally involve:

Selecting the Right Software: Choose a program or language appropriate for the import process (e.g., spreadsheet applications like Excel, programming languages like Python or R).

Reading the CSV File:

In Excel, use the "Import" functionality found under the "Data" tab.

In Python, utilize libraries like `pandas` with functions like `pd.read_csv('file.csv')` to load the data into a DataFrame.

Handling Delimiters: Ensure the correct delimiter is set, as some CSV files may use tabs or semi-colons instead of commas.

Data Cleaning: After the import, review the dataset for inconsistencies, missing values, or data type errors, and address them as necessary.

6.3.2 Importing from Excel Files

Importing from Excel files involves similar steps but may require additional considerations due to the formatting options within Excel:

Tool Selection: Use applications like Excel or programming libraries such as `openpyxl` or `pandas` (e.g., `pd.read_excel('file.xlsx')`).

Navigating Worksheets: If your Excel file contains multiple sheets, specify which sheet to import, either by name or index.

Handling Data Types: Excel can store data in various formats, so ensure that numeric and date fields are correctly interpreted.

Cleaning Up Imported Data: Similar to CSV import, always verify the integrity of the imported data and check for any formatting issues.

6.4 Exporting Data

6.4.1 Exporting to CSV Files

When exporting data to CSV files, maintain a clear and straightforward process:

Select the Export Option: In spreadsheets, use the "Save As" option and choose CSV as the file type.

Check for Proper Formatting: Ensure data types are converted appropriately, and formatting is simplified, as CSV does not support rich formatting.

Encoding Considerations: Save the file with an appropriate encoding (e.g., UTF-8) to ensure compatibility with different systems.

Testing Import Functionality: After exporting, consider re-importing the CSV file into your original software to test the integrity of the data.

6.4.2 Exporting to Excel Files

Exporting to Excel allows for more extensive data manipulation options:

Export to Excel Format: Many applications include direct export options to create Excel files, which are often found in the "File" menu.

Customize Formatting: Take the opportunity to apply formatting such as colors, styles, and formulas before exporting to enhance readability and usability.

Saving Multiple Sheets: If exporting complex datasets, remember that Excel allows the creation of multiple sheets. Organize data accordingly.

Review and Test: Just as with CSV, ensure to recheck the Excel files for discrepancies after export—ensuring all data is present and correctly formatted.

6.5 Best Practices

Data Validation: Always validate the data integrity during both import and export processes. Use checks and controls to identify discrepancies.

Documentation: Maintain clear documentation regarding the data sources, file structures, and transformation processes used during import/export.

Regular Backups: Keep backups of original and processed data to prevent any loss during manipulation.

Consistent Naming Conventions: Use clear and consistent naming for files to ensure easy identification and retrieval.

These skills facilitate not only effective data handling but also enable seamless collaboration between stakeholders with diverse software environments. By adopting best practices and understanding the strengths and limitations of each file format, you can ensure data integrity and optimize your analytical processes. As we move forward, the emphasis on proficient data management will be crucial in an increasingly data-driven world.

Reading and Writing CSV Files with Python

Python, a versatile and powerful programming language, provides a variety of libraries that make it easy to work with CSV files. This chapter will cover how to read from and write to CSV files using Python's built-in

`csv` module as well as the popular `pandas` library, enabling you to manipulate data effectively for various applications.

Understanding CSV Format

A CSV file consists of rows and columns, where each row represents a record and each column an attribute of that record. The values in each row are separated by a comma, although other delimiters such as semicolons or tabs can also be used.

Example of a CSV file

```plaintext
name,age,city Alice,30,New York Bob,25,Los Angeles Charlie,35,Chicago
```

Each line in the above file corresponds to a different person, with their name, age, and city of residence separated by commas.

Reading CSV Files

Using the `csv` Module

The `csv` module in Python allows you to read CSV files easily. You can utilize the `csv.reader` function to read data from a CSV file.

Sample Code

```python import csv
# Reading CSV file
```

with open('data.csv', mode='r') as file: csv_reader = csv.reader(file)

```
# Skip the header row if necessary next(csv_reader)
```

for row in csv_reader: print(row)
```
```

In this example, we open a CSV file named `data.csv`, create a CSV reader object, skip the header row, and print each subsequent row.

Using `pandas`

The `pandas` library provides a powerful and flexible way to read and manipulate CSV files. With `pandas`, you can load CSV data into a DataFrame, which is a 2-dimensional labeled data structure similar to a table.

Sample Code

```python
import pandas as pd
# Reading CSV file
df = pd.read_csv('data.csv')
# Display the DataFrame print(df)
```
```
```

By using `pd.read_csv()`, we can easily read a CSV file into a DataFrame, enabling advanced data manipulation capabilities.

Writing CSV Files

Using the `csv` Module

To write data to a CSV file using the `csv` module, you can use `csv.writer`. #### Sample Code

```python
import csv
# Writing to CSV file data = [
['name', 'age', 'city'],
['Alice', 30, 'New York'],
['Bob', 25, 'Los Angeles'],
['Charlie', 35, 'Chicago']
]
with open('output.csv', mode='w', newline='') as file:
csv_writer = csv.writer(file) csv_writer.writerows(data)
```

This code snippet creates a new CSV file named `output.csv` and writes the specified data, including the header.

Using `pandas`

Just like reading, writing a CSV file with `pandas` is straightforward using `DataFrame.to_csv()`. #### Sample Code

```python
```

```python
import pandas as pd
# Creating a DataFrame data = {
'name': ['Alice', 'Bob', 'Charlie'], 'age': [30, 25, 35],
'city': ['New York', 'Los Angeles', 'Chicago']
}
df = pd.DataFrame(data) # Writing to CSV file
df.to_csv('output_pandas.csv', index=False)
```

This code creates a DataFrame and writes it to a new CSV file named `output_pandas.csv`, omitting the index for cleaner output.

Handling CSV Files with Different Delimiters

In some cases, CSV files may use delimiters other than commas. Both the `csv` module and `pandas` can handle this easily.

Using the `csv` Module

```python
import csv

with open('data.tsv', mode='r') as file:

csv_reader = csv.reader(file, delimiter='\t') # Using tab as a delimiter for row in csv_reader:

print(row)
```

Using `pandas`

```python
import pandas as pd
```

```
df = pd.read_csv('data.tsv', sep='\t')  # Using tab as a
separator print(df)
```
```

We learned how to handle CSV data efficiently, manipulate tables, and work with various delimiters. CSV files are a fundamental tool for data storage and transfer, and mastering their usage in Python opens the door to effective data analysis and manipulation. In the subsequent chapters, we will delve deeper into data analysis techniques and how to apply them using the skills we have developed here.

## Handling Excel Files and Data Validation

With its user-friendly interface and powerful capabilities, it empowers users across industries to perform complex tasks. For Python developers, the integration of Excel functionalities into their workflows opens up new horizons in data manipulation and analysis. This chapter is dedicated to exploring how Python can be utilized to handle Excel files effectively while ensuring data integrity through validation techniques.

## 5.1 Introduction to Pandas and Openpyxl

Before diving into specific techniques for handling Excel files, it is essential to become familiar with two key libraries: **Pandas** and **Openpyxl**.

### 5.1.1 Pandas

Pandas is an open-source data analysis library that provides data structures and functions needed to manipulate numerical tables and time series. Most importantly, Pandas includes powerful functions for
```

reading and writing Excel files.

5.1.2 Openpyxl

Openpyxl is another popular library that specifically focuses on reading and writing Excel 2010 xlsx/xlsm/xltx/xltm files. While Pandas is great for general data analysis, Openpyxl allows for more advanced Excel-specific functionalities, such as formatting cells, applying styles, and creating charts.

To get started with these libraries, you can install them using pip:

```bash
pip install pandas openpyxl
```

5.2 Reading and Writing Excel Files ### 5.2.1 Reading Excel Files with Pandas

Pandas provides a straightforward method to read Excel files using the `read_excel()` function. Here's how you can read data from an Excel file:

```python
import pandas as pd

# Read an Excel file
df = pd.read_excel('data.xlsx', sheet_name='Sheet1')

# Display the first few rows print(df.head())
```

5.2.2 Writing Data to Excel Files

Writing data back to an Excel file is just as simple. You

can use the `to_excel()` method:

```python
# Write DataFrame to an Excel file
df.to_excel('output.xlsx',                    index=False,
sheet_name='OutputSheet')
```

This command writes the DataFrame to an Excel file called `output.xlsx`, without including the index. ## 5.3 Data Validation Techniques

Data validation is crucial in ensuring that the data being collected is accurate and meets the required standards. In this section, we will discuss methods to perform data validation on Excel files using Python.

5.3.1 Basic Data Validation

Basic data validation involves checking for null or missing values, ensuring data types are correct, and confirming that values fall within a specific range. Here is an example of how to validate a DataFrame:

```python
# Validate for missing values if df.isnull().values.any():

print("Data contains missing values!")

# Validate data types

if not pd.api.types.is_numeric_dtype(df['column_name']):

print("Invalid data type in column_name!")

# Validate a range for numerical values

if not df['numeric_column'].between(0, 100).all():

print("Values in numeric_column are out of range!")
```

```
```

5.3.2 Advanced Data Validation with Openpyxl

For more advanced validation, such as dropdown lists or specific formatting, Openpyxl offers robust capabilities. You can apply data validation directly in the Excel file as follows:

```python
from openpyxl import Workbook

from openpyxl.worksheet.datavalidation import DataValidation

# Create a workbook and select the active sheet wb = Workbook()

ws = wb.active

# Create a data validation object for dropdown

dv = DataValidation(type="list", formula1="'Option1,Option2,Option3'", showDropDown=True)

# Add data validation to cells ws.add_data_validation(dv)

dv.add('A1:A10')  # Applying dropdown to cell range A1 to A10

# Save the workbook wb.save('data_with_validation.xlsx')
```

This script creates an Excel file with dropdown options in cells A1 through A10, allowing users to select from pre-defined choices, thus minimizing human error.

5.3.3 Custom Data Validation Functions

In scenarios where criteria are more complex, custom validation functions can be defined in Python. For instance, you could create a function that checks if all emails in a column are formatted correctly:

```python
import re

def validate_emails(email_series):
    email_pattern = r'^[\w\.-]+@[\w\.-]+\.\w+$'
    invalid_emails = email_series[~email_series.str.match(email_pattern)]
    return invalid_emails

invalid_emails = validate_emails(df['email_column'])
if not invalid_emails.empty:
    print(f"Invalid emails found:\n{invalid_emails}")
```

Handling Excel files and performing data validation with Python not only eases the workflow but also enhances data integrity and accuracy. With libraries like Pandas and Openpyxl, you can manipulate Excel files seamlessly, while robust validation techniques ensure that the data collected adheres to required standards. In the next chapter, we will explore how to visualize this validated data effectively to derive meaningful insights.

Chapter 7: Combining Data from Multiple Sources

In this chapter, we will explore the methodologies and Python tools that allow data professionals to combine data from multiple sources effectively. We will leverage popular libraries, including `pandas`, `numpy`, and `sqlite3`, to perform data merging, concatenation, and integration tasks. ## 7.1 Understanding Data Sources

Before diving into code, it is essential to understand the different types of data sources you may encounter. Data can come from various formats and locations, such as:

CSV files: Simple and widely used for storing tabular data.

SQL databases: Structured data stored in relational databases.

APIs: Data fetched from web services in JSON or XML formats.

Excel spreadsheets: Popular in business environments for data analysis.

NoSQL databases: Such as MongoDB, for unstructured or semi-structured data.

A comprehensive approach requires identifying these sources and understanding their structures. ### Example Data Sources

In our examples, we'll work with the following fictional datasets:

Employees (CSV): a list of employees with attributes like ID, name, and department.

Departments (SQL Database): a table containing department IDs and names.

Salaries (JSON API): an API providing salaries linked to employee IDs. ## 7.2 Loading Data from Various Sources

Loading CSV Files

To begin, let's utilize the `pandas` library to load our employee dataset from a CSV file.

```python
import pandas as pd

# Load CSV file

employees = pd.read_csv('employees.csv')
print(employees.head())
```

Loading Data from SQL Databases

Next, we will connect to an SQLite database to load the departments.

```python
import sqlite3

# Connect to the SQLite database
conn = sqlite3.connect('company.db')
```

```python
# Load Departments table
departments = pd.read_sql_query('SELECT * FROM departments', conn) print(departments.head())
```

Loading Data from JSON API

Let's fetch salary information from a fictional API using the `requests` library.

```python
import requests

# Fetch JSON data from API
response = requests.get('https://api.example.com/salaries') salaries = pd.json_normalize(response.json()) print(salaries.head())
```

7.3 Merging DataFrames

Once we have our datasets ready, we can merge them based on common columns. In this scenario, we will use the employee ID from the `employees` dataframe to join with the `salaries` dataframe.

Using `merge`

The `merge` function in `pandas` is powerful for combining datasets based on a key. Here is how we can perform the merge:

```python
# Merge employees with salaries on employee ID
employee_salaries = pd.merge(employees, salaries,
```

```python
                    on='employee_id',                    how='inner')
print(employee_salaries.head())
```

Merging with Multiple DataFrames

We can continue merging the resulting DataFrame with the `departments` DataFrame to enrich our dataset further.

```python
# Merge with departments on department ID

final_dataset       =       pd.merge(employee_salaries, departments,      on='department_id',      how='left')
print(final_dataset.head())
```

7.4 Concatenating DataFrames

In some cases, you might need to stack datasets vertically. For instance, if you have multiple `CSV` files for employees in different regions, you can concatenate them easily.

```python
# Assuming we have multiple CSV files

regional_employees                              =
pd.concat([pd.read_csv('region1_employees.csv'),
pd.read_csv('region2_employees.csv')],
```

ignore_index=True) print(regional_employees.head())
```

## 7.5 Handling Data Quality Issues

As we bring data from multiple sources, it's crucial to inspect and clean the resulting dataset. Common issues include missing values, duplicates, and inconsistencies. Here are some strategies to address these problems:

### Identifying Missing Values

```python print(final_dataset.isnull().sum())
```

Filling Missing Values

```python

# Fill missing values with a default value or using interpolation
final_dataset['salary'].fillna(final_dataset['salary'].mean(), inplace=True)
```

Dropping Duplicates

```python final_dataset.drop_duplicates(inplace=True)
```

7.6 Exporting the Combined Dataset

After combining and cleaning, the next step is to export your final dataset for future use or analysis.

```python

# Export to a new CSV
final_dataset.to_csv('combined_employee_data.csv',

index=False)
```
` ` `
```

Combining data from multiple sources is a fundamental skill in data analysis that allows organizations to obtain a holistic view of their operations. By leveraging Python's libraries such as `pandas`, `sqlite3`, and

`requests`, you can effectively manage and synthesize data regardless of its origin.

Merging Data from Different APIs and Databases

Many organizations rely on several APIs and databases to gather information, leading to the necessity to merge this data for analysis and decision-making. This chapter focuses on the process of merging data from different APIs and databases using Python, a versatile programming language renowned for its capability in data manipulation and analysis.

Understanding the Basics

Before diving into the coding aspects, it's crucial to understand what is meant by APIs and databases.

APIs (Application Programming Interfaces) are sets of rules and protocols for building and interacting with software applications. APIs allow different software entities to communicate with each other, enabling data exchange.

Databases are structured collections of data stored electronically. Common databases include SQL- based systems like MySQL, PostgreSQL, and NoSQL systems like MongoDB.

Merging data from these sources involves fetching data from APIs, querying databases, and then integrating these data sets into a single coherent structure.

Tools and Libraries

To effectively merge data from various sources, you will utilize several Python libraries:

Requests: For sending HTTP requests to APIs and retrieving data.

Pandas: For data manipulation and analysis, including merging datasets.

SQLAlchemy: For database connections and queries.

JSON: For parsing JSON data from APIs.

Make sure to install these libraries if you haven't already:

```bash

pip install requests pandas sqlalchemy

```

Step 1: Fetching Data from an API

Let's start with fetching data from a sample API. For this example, we'll use the JSONPlaceholder API, a free REST API for testing and prototyping.

```python
import requests

import pandas as pd

# Fetching data from the API

response = requests.get('https://jsonplaceholder.typicode.com/posts') posts_data = response.json()
```

```
# Convert to a DataFrame
posts_df = pd.DataFrame(posts_data)
print(posts_df.head())
```

Step 2: Querying a Database

Next, let's simulate fetching data from a SQL database. You would typically set up a database connection using SQLAlchemy. For example, we'll connect to a hypothetical SQLite database.

```python
from sqlalchemy import create_engine

# Create a database connection
engine = create_engine('sqlite:///example.db')  # replace with your database URL

# Querying the database
users_df = pd.read_sql('SELECT * FROM users', con=engine) print(users_df.head())
```

Step 3: Merging the Data

Now that we have data from both the API and the database, we can merge these two DataFrames using Pandas. Assume that both datasets contain a common identifier, such as `userId`.

```python
# Merging the DataFrames
merged_df = pd.merge(posts_df, users_df,
```

left_on='userId', right_on='id') print(merged_df.head())
```

### Handling Data Types and Missing Values

When merging different data sources, it is essential to ensure that the data types are compatible and handle any missing values appropriately. Use the `fillna` and `astype` methods from Pandas to address these issues.

```python
# Filling missing values

merged_df.fillna({'name': 'Unknown', 'email': 'unknown@example.com'}, inplace=True)

# Converting data types if necessary merged_df['userId'] = merged_df['userId'].astype(int)
```

Step 4: Analyzing and Visualizing Merged Data

The merged DataFrame is now ready for analysis. You can perform various operations like grouping, aggregating, and visualizing the data.

```python
# Example analysis: Counting posts per user

posts_per_user = merged_df.groupby('name')['title'].count().reset_index() print(posts_per_user)

# Visualizing the result

import matplotlib.pyplot as plt
```
```

```
plt.bar(posts_per_user['name'],    posts_per_user['title'])
plt.xlabel('User Name')
```

```
plt.ylabel('Number  of  Posts')  plt.title('Posts  per  User')
plt.xticks(rotation=45) plt.show()
```
```

Merging data from different APIs and databases can significantly enhance your analysis capabilities. By following the steps outlined in this chapter—fetching data, querying databases, merging datasets, and performing analysis—you can create a robust workflow for consolidating information. Python's extensive libraries make this process not only feasible but also efficient, enabling you to focus on gaining insights from your data rather than struggling with integration issues.

## Data Cleaning and Transformation Techniques

Data cleaning is a critical step in any data analysis or data science project. It ensures that your dataset is accurate, consistent, and usable for analysis. In this chapter, we will explore various techniques for data cleaning using Python, one of the most popular programming languages for data science. We will utilize libraries such as Pandas, NumPy, and Matplotlib to facilitate the data cleaning process.

## 1. Understanding Data Cleaning

Before diving into the techniques, it's essential to understand what data cleaning involves. Data cleaning is the process of identifying and correcting (or removing) inaccurate records from a dataset. Cleaning can include:

Handling missing values

Removing duplicates
```

Correcting data types

Standardizing formats

Detecting outliers

Let's break down these techniques with examples using Python. ## 2. Setting Up Your Environment

To begin, you'll need to install the necessary libraries if you haven't already. The most commonly used libraries for data manipulation in Python are Pandas and NumPy. You may also use Matplotlib for visualization.

```bash
pip install pandas numpy matplotlib
```

Then, import these libraries in your Python script or Jupyter Notebook:

```python
import pandas as pd import numpy as np

import matplotlib.pyplot as plt
```

3. Loading Data

Let's assume you have a dataset in CSV format. You can load your data into a Pandas DataFrame as follows:

```python
data = pd.read_csv('your_dataset.csv')
```

4. Exploring the Dataset

Before cleaning, it's vital to understand the structure and content of your data:

```python
print(data.head())
print(data.info())
print(data.describe())
```

5. Handling Missing Values

Missing values can occur for various reasons and can significantly impact your analysis. Pandas provides several techniques to handle them:

5.1 Identifying Missing Values

You can easily check for missing values using the `isnull()` function:

```python
print(data.isnull().sum())
```

5.2 Removing Missing Values

If a row contains too many missing values, you might consider dropping it:

```python
data_cleaned = data.dropna()
```

5.3 Filling Missing Values

Alternatively, you may want to fill in missing values using a specific strategy, such as the mean, median, or a specific value:

```python
data['column_name'].fillna(data['column_name'].mean(),
```
114

inplace=True)
```

## 6. Removing Duplicates

Duplicate records can lead to skewed results. You can check for duplicates and remove them as follows:

```python print(data.duplicated().sum()) data_cleaned =
data.drop_duplicates()
```

7. Correcting Data Types

Data types can often be misinterpreted, especially when importing data. Use the `dtypes` property to inspect the types:

```python print(data.dtypes)
```

Convert data types where necessary:

```python
data['column_name'] = data['column_name'].astype(int)
```

8. Standardizing Formats

Standardizing formats—such as date formats or string casing—is another essential step. For example, you can standardize date formats using:

```python
data['date_column']                            =
pd.to_datetime(data['date_column'])
```
```

```
```

You can also standardize string formats (e.g., converting to lowercase):

```python
data['string_column'] = data['string_column'].str.lower()
```

9. Detecting and Handling Outliers

Outliers can distort your analysis. Using visualization techniques, such as box plots or histograms, can help identify outliers:

```python
plt.boxplot(data['numeric_column']) plt.show()
```

After identification, you can choose to remove or cap these values:

```python
data_cleaned = data[(data['numeric_column'] < upper_bound) & (data['numeric_column'] > lower_bound)]
```

10. Final Thoughts

Data cleaning is iterative and may require multiple passes to ensure the dataset is clean and ready for analysis. It's important to document your cleaning process to maintain transparency and reproducibility in your analyses.

By employing these techniques, you can transform messy datasets into clean, structured data that is ready for analysis, visualization, or model building. Mastery of data cleaning techniques in Python is essential for any aspiring data scientist or analyst, and the skills you cultivate in this process will serve as a fundamental aspect of your data manipulation toolkit.

Chapter 8: Real-Time Data Integration

Real-time data integration is crucial for applications that require quick responses to changing conditions, such as financial trading platforms, social media monitoring, and e-commerce personalization. In this chapter, we will explore how to leverage Python to implement real-time data integration, using libraries and tools that facilitate data ingestion, processing, and storage.

1. Understanding Real-Time Data Integration

Real-time data integration involves combining data from various sources into a unified view as the data is produced. This process often requires handling streams of data generated from different applications or sensors. The challenge lies in ensuring that the data flow is seamless, up-to-date, and reliable.

1.1 Key Concepts

Data Sources: These can range from databases and APIs to IoT devices and message queues.

Data Streams: Continuous flows of data generated in real time that must be processed and analyzed immediately.

Event-Driven Architecture: A system design pattern that invokes actions in response to events, suitable for real-time processing.

2. Common Use Cases

Financial Services: Implementing real-time alerts for trading based on price fluctuations.

Retail: Real-time inventory management systems that

automatically update stock levels as sales occur.

Healthcare: Monitoring patient vitals that trigger immediate alerts to medical staff.

Social Media Analytics: Tracking and analyzing mentions and sentiments in real-time. ## 3. Tools and Libraries

Python provides a rich ecosystem of libraries to facilitate real-time data integration:

Apache Kafka: A distributed streaming platform that can publish and subscribe to streams of records.

Pandas: Although commonly used for data manipulation and analysis, it can help process batch transformations on data streams.

Streamlit: Useful for building data applications quickly and easily for real-time data visualization.

Tornado: An asynchronous networking library for building scalable network applications. ## 4. Designing a Real-Time Data Pipeline

Designing a real-time data pipeline involves four main phases:

4.1 Data Ingestion

Data ingestion is the first step in the pipeline. It can be achieved using multiple methods:

Message Brokers: Tools like Kafka and RabbitMQ allow you to publish and subscribe to data streams efficiently.

Webhooks: HTTP callbacks that push data to your application in real time. #### Example: Data Ingestion

Using Kafka

```python
from kafka import KafkaConsumer
# Set up a Kafka consumer consumer = KafkaConsumer(
'my_topic',                bootstrap_servers='localhost:9092',
auto_offset_reset='earliest', enable_auto_commit=True,
group_id='my-group'
)
for message in consumer:
print(f"Received: {message.value.decode('utf-8')}")
```

4.2 Data Processing

Once data is ingested, it must be processed to convert it into a usable format. Use Python libraries like Pandas or NumPy for this purpose.

Example: Data Processing with Pandas

```python
import pandas as pd import json
def process_data(data):
df = pd.DataFrame(data) # Perform transformations
df['timestamp'] = pd.to_datetime(df['timestamp']) return df
```

4.3 Data Storage

Processed data needs to be stored for future analysis. Depending on the use case, either a relational database or a NoSQL database may be suitable.

Example of using PostgreSQL with SQLAlchemy:

```python
from sqlalchemy import create_engine

engine = create_engine('postgresql://user:password@localhost/db name') # Store processed data

df.to_sql('my_table', engine, if_exists='append', index=False)
```

4.4 Data Visualization

Visualizing real-time data enables users to make sense of information quickly. Streamlit is a fantastic tool to create interactive dashboards.

Example: Building a Basic Streamlit App

```python
import streamlit as st import pandas as pd
# Assume 'df' is your DataFrame containing the latest data
st.title('Real-Time Data Dashboard')
st.dataframe(df)
```

5. Challenges in Real-Time Data Integration

As with any system, integrating real-time data comes with challenges:

Data Quality: Ensuring accuracy and completeness in data streams is crucial.

Latency: Minimizing latency in data processing and delivery is key to effective real-time applications.

Scalability: Designing the system to handle large volumes of incoming data without bottlenecks is critical.

Error Handling: Implementing robust error-handling mechanisms to deal with data discrepancies or service outages.

Real-time data integration is vital for organizations looking to stay competitive in a fast-paced, data-driven environment. Python's rich ecosystem of libraries and frameworks allows developers to build flexible and scalable data pipelines that cater to various real-time use cases. By focusing on robust design, efficient processing, and effective visualization, developers can unlock the full potential of real-time data. As you continue your journey through data integration, embrace the challenges, and leverage the power of Python to innovate and optimize your applications.

Implementing Real-Time Data Fetching in Excel with Python

Microsoft Excel remains one of the most popular tools for data analysis, but it often relies on static data sets. With the integration of Python, users can leverage the power of real-time data fetching, allowing for dynamic dashboards and live updates. This chapter will guide you through implementing real-time data fetching in Excel using Python, enhancing your Excel spreadsheet with up-to-the-minute information.

Understanding the Prerequisites

Before diving into implementation, ensure you have the following prerequisites:

Microsoft Excel: Ensure you have a recent version of Excel installed on your computer.

Python Installation: Install Python from [python.org](https://www.python.org). It's advisable to use Python 3.x.

Libraries: You will need several libraries, including `pandas`, `requests`, and `openpyxl`. Use pip to install these libraries if you haven't done so already:

```bash
pip install pandas requests openpyxl
```

Excel and Python Integration: You can utilize the `xlwings` library to connect Python with Excel seamlessly. Install it using pip:

```bash
pip install xlwings
```

API Access: Get access to a third-party API that provides real-time data, such as stock prices, weather information, or cryptocurrency values. For this guide, we will use the Alpha Vantage API, which provides free access to financial data.

Setting Up the Environment ### API Key Registration

First, you need to register for an API key with Alpha Vantage:

Visit the [Alpha Vantage](https://www.alphavantage.co/support/#api-key) website.

Sign up for a free account and obtain your API key. ### Creating the Python Script

Create a new Python script (`real_time_data.py`) for fetching and returning data. Below is a simple example of how to fetch stock price data using `requests`:

```python
import requests

import pandas as pd
```

```
def fetch_stock_data(symbol):

api_key = 'YOUR_API_KEY' url =
f'https://www.alphavantage.co/query?function=TIME_SE
RIES_INTRADAY&symbol={symbol}&interval=1min&a

response = requests.get(url) data = response.json()
# Extract the latest data
time_series = data['Time Series (1min)'] latest_timestamp
=   sorted(time_series.keys())[0]   latest_data   =
time_series[latest_timestamp]

return pd.DataFrame({ 'Symbol': [symbol], 'Time':
[latest_timestamp],
'Open': [latest_data['1. open']],
'High': [latest_data['2. high']],
'Low': [latest_data['3. low']],
'Close': [latest_data['4. close']], 'Volume': [latest_data['5.
volume']]
})
```
```

Replace `'YOUR_API_KEY'` with the actual API key you received from Alpha Vantage. ## Integrating with Excel

### Setting Up the Excel File

Open Microsoft Excel and create a new workbook.

In the first row, input the column headers: `Symbol`,
```

`Time`, `Open`, `High`, `Low`, `Close`, `Volume`. ### Using xlwings

Now we'll set up a function in Python that allows us to call the data-fetching script from Excel:

```python
import xlwings as xw

@xw.func

def get_stock_info(symbol):

return fetch_stock_data(symbol)
```

Running the Function

In the same directory as `real_time_data.py`, create an Excel file `RealTimeStockData.xlsx`.

In the cell A2 of your Excel file, enter a stock symbol (e.g., `AAPL` for Apple).

In cell B2, you can invoke the custom Python function as follows:

```excel
=get_stock_info(A2)
```

Refreshing the Data

To ensure that your data is updated in real time, you can set up a Macro in Excel to refresh the data periodically:

Press `Alt + F11` to open the VBA editor.

Insert a new module and write a function to refresh:

```vba
Sub RefreshData() Application.CalculateFull
End Sub
```

You can assign this macro to a button or set it to run at regular intervals using the `Application.OnTime` method.

By utilizing APIs and automating data retrieval, analysts can monitor important metrics dynamically. The simplicity and flexibility of Python paired with Excel's familiar interface allow for powerful analytical tools to be developed easily. As you explore further, consider integrating additional data sources or customizing your Python functions to suit specific analytical requirements. The real-time capabilities you establish will serve as the foundation for more advanced data analysis and business intelligence in your organization.

Updating Excel Workbooks with Live Data

However, static data can quickly become obsolete in dynamic environments. Therefore, incorporating live data updates into Excel workbooks presents a powerful solution for professionals across various fields. This chapter explores techniques for integrating live data with Excel, ensuring that your spreadsheets reflect the most current information available, enhancing accuracy, and improving decision-making.

1. Understanding Live Data in Excel

Live data refers to information that can be updated in real-time or near real-time as changes occur in its source. This data can come from various sources, including databases, online services, APIs, stock exchanges, and even other Excel files. By connecting your Excel workbook to live data sources, you create a dynamic report that evolves alongside the information it represents.

Key Features of Live Data Integration:

Automatic Updates: Changes in the data source can be reflected in Excel with minimal manual intervention.

Real-Time Reporting: Users can monitor changing metrics and KPIs continuously.

Improved Accuracy: Reduces the risk of using outdated information, leading to better-informed decisions.

2. Methods for Importing Live Data

There are various methods to pull live data into Excel, each suited for different types of data sources. Here are some of the most common techniques:

2.1. Connecting to Online Data Sources

Excel offers built-in features to link with various web-based data sources. To get started:

Using Power Query: This tool allows users to connect to a wide array of data sources, including websites and REST APIs.

Go to the `Data` tab and select `Get Data`.

Choose `From Other Sources` > `From Web`.

Enter the URL of the data source to connect, transform,

and load the data into Excel.

Web Queries: For simple tables or data lists on web pages, you can use web queries.

Select `Data` > `Get Data` > `From Web` and follow the prompts to set up a query that pulls data directly from a webpage.

2.2. Connecting to Databases

If you are working with organizational databases, Excel can seamlessly connect to them to fetch live data using ODBC (Open Database Connectivity) or OLE DB (Object Linking and Embedding Database).

Accessing Databases:

Go to `Data` > `Get Data` > `From Database` and select your database type (e.g., SQL Server, Access, etc.).

Input the necessary connection information, such as server and database names.

Create queries as needed to extract relevant tables or datasets.

2.3. Using External APIs

Many modern applications and services expose their data through APIs. Utilizing APIs in Excel allows for more complex data sets, including JSON and XML formats.

1. **Connecting via Power Query**:

- As with online sources, you can use `Power Query` to pull in data from APIs. Enter the API endpoint in the

`From Web` dialog, and if authentication is required, follow the prompts to enter your credentials.

2.4. Streaming Data from Excel Add-Ins

Excel's ecosystem includes numerous add-ins that facilitate live data integration. For example, financial data providers may offer Excel add-ins that deliver real-time stock quotes or market indices directly into worksheets.

3. Refreshing Live Data

To ensure that your Excel workbook displays the most up-to-date information, configuring data refresh settings is essential:

3.1. Manual Refresh

You can manually refresh the data connection at any time by:

Selecting the `Data` tab and clicking `Refresh All`.

Using shortcuts (e.g., `Ctrl + Alt + F5`) to quickly refresh.
3.2. Automatic Refresh

Excel also allows you to set automatic refresh intervals:

Access the connection properties by selecting `Data` > `Queries & Connections`.

Right-click the desired connection and select `Properties`.

In the properties window, enable `Refresh every X minutes` and specify your timeframe. ## 4. Case Studies

Case Study 1: Financial Analysis

A financial analyst at a multinational company developing financial models linked to live market data automatically updates every hour. By integrating stock market feeds into their Excel workbooks, they can provide accurate, real-time insights into asset prices and perform scenario analysis effectively.

Case Study 2: Sales Dashboard

A sales manager utilizes a dashboard in Excel linked to their CRM system via API. This connection allows the sales team to monitor the status of deals, sales figures, and performance metrics in real-time, enabling better strategic decisions and timely interventions.

By understanding the methods to connect and refresh data, professionals can leverage the full power of Excel to make informed decisions based on real-time information. As technology continues to advance, the ability to incorporate live data will remain a critical skill for anyone looking to succeed in data-driven environments. Embrace these techniques to ensure your Excel workbooks are always reflecting the most current data available.

Chapter 9: Automating Data Integration Processes with Python

This chapter explores how Python can be leveraged to automate data integration processes, offering robust solutions to streamline workflows and enhance data quality.

Understanding Data Integration

Data integration involves combining data from different sources into a unified view, allowing organizations to analyze their data comprehensively. The sources can range from databases, APIs, and flat files to web scraping. This chapter will cover the concepts of data integration and the challenges that may arise during the process, such as data format mismatches, data cleansing, and transformation discrepancies.

Key Concepts in Data Integration

ETL Process: The Extract, Transform, Load (ETL) framework is a traditional approach to data integration. Python can be a powerful tool to automate each stage of this process.

Data Sources: Understanding the types of data sources (SQL databases, NoSQL databases, APIs, CSV files, etc.) is crucial for designing an effective integration strategy.

APIs: Many data sources provide APIs for easier access. Knowing how to interact with these APIs is essential for retrieving data efficiently.

Data Quality: Maintaining the quality of data involves validation, cleansing, and ensuring consistency across merged datasets.

Setting Up Your Environment

Before automating data integration, ensure you have the necessary Python packages installed:

```bash
pip install pandas sqlalchemy requests
```

Pandas: A powerful library for data manipulation and analysis.

SQLAlchemy: A toolkit for SQL database access.

Requests: A library for making HTTP requests to APIs. ## Extracting Data

The first step in the ETL process is extraction. Depending on the source, the approach to extraction will differ.

Extracting Data from SQL Databases

Using SQLAlchemy, you can extract data from a SQL database as follows:

```python
from sqlalchemy import create_engine import pandas as pd

# Create a database connection string

engine                  = create_engine('mysql+pymysql://username:password@host:port/database')


# Query to extract data
```

```
query = "SELECT * FROM your_table_name"
```

```
# Load the data into a DataFrame df = pd.read_sql(query,
engine)
```

Extracting Data from APIs

To extract data from a RESTful API, you can use the Requests library:

```python
import requests
```

```
# Define the API endpoint
```

```
url = "https://api.example.com/data"
```

```
# Send the request  response = requests.get(url) data =
response.json()
```

```
# Convert to DataFrame if necessary df_api =
pd.DataFrame(data)
```

Transforming Data

Data extracted from multiple sources may not align perfectly. Transformation is where data wrangling comes into play.

Standardizing Data Formats

For example, if you are merging data from two sources with date fields in different formats, you can standardize them using `pandas`:

```python
df['date_column'] = pd.to_datetime(df['date_column'],
format='%Y-%m-%d')
```

```
```

Data Cleaning

Addressing missing values and duplicates is crucial for high-quality data:

```python
# Removing duplicates df.drop_duplicates(inplace=True)
```

Filling missing values df.fillna(method='ffill', inplace=True)
```
```

Loading Data

Once the data has been cleaned and transformed, it's time to load the data into the desired destination, be it another database, a CSV file, or a data warehouse.

Loading Data into SQL

To load data back into a SQL database, use the `to_sql` method from pandas:

```python
df.to_sql('new_table_name',                    con=engine,
if_exists='replace', index=False)
```
```

### Saving Data to CSV

For simpler tasks, you may opt to save the cleaned data to a CSV file:

```python
```
```

```python
df.to_csv('cleaned_data.csv', index=False)
```

Automating the Process

To make the entire process automated, you can encapsulate the ETL workflow in a function or a script.

```python
def automate_etl():
# Extract
df_sql = pd.read_sql("SELECT * FROM your_table_name", engine) response = requests.get(url)
df_api = pd.DataFrame(response.json())


# Transform
df_sql['date_column'] = pd.to_datetime(df_sql['date_column'])
df_sql.drop_duplicates(inplace=True)


# Load
df_sql.to_sql('new_table_name', con=engine, if_exists='replace', index=False)
if __name__ == "__main__":
automate_etl()
```

Scheduling with Cron Jobs or Task Scheduler

To run your automation script at scheduled intervals,

137

consider using Cron on Unix-based systems or Task Scheduler on Windows. A basic Cron job to run the script daily at midnight would look like:

```bash
0 0 * * * /usr/bin/python3 /path/to/your/script.py
```

Error Handling

Automation without error handling can lead to failures. Implement try-except blocks to manage exceptions effectively:

```python
try:
```

Your ETL operations here except Exception as e:

print(f"An error occurred: {e}")

```
```

Automating data integration processes with Python can significantly reduce manual workload, enhance accuracy, and facilitate more timely decision-making based on analytical insights. As this chapter illustrated, the combination of Python libraries and strategic planning can create effective data pipelines. In the following chapters, we will delve deeper into advanced data integration techniques and how to ensure the security and compliance of your automated processes.

Scheduling Python Scripts for Regular Data Updates

One of the key challenges that data professionals face is ensuring that their data is always up-to-date. Regular data updates can be critical for many applications, from dashboards displaying real-time information to ETL (Extract, Transform, Load) processes that feed into data warehouses. In this chapter, we will explore how to schedule Python scripts to automate data updates, allowing for a seamless flow of data while minimizing manual intervention.

1. Understanding the Need for Automation

Automation in data processing has numerous advantages. It:

Reduces manual errors.

Saves time and resources.

Ensures consistency in data updates.

Provides timely data for analytics and reporting.

By scheduling Python scripts, you can set up automated workflows that run at specific intervals, gathering data from various sources, processing it, and storing it for analysis.

2. Choosing the Right Scheduling Tool

There are several tools and methods available for scheduling Python scripts, each with its own strengths and use cases. Here are some popular ones:

2.1. Cron (Linux/Mac)

Cron is a time-based job scheduler in Unix-like operating systems. It allows users to schedule scripts or commands at specific intervals (minutely, hourly, daily, weekly, etc.).

Example: Scheduling a Python Script with Cron

Open the terminal and type `crontab -e` to edit the cron jobs.

Add a new line for your scheduled task. For example, to run the script `update_data.py` every day at midnight:
```

0      0      *      *      *        /usr/bin/python3 /path/to/your/script/update_data.py
```

```
```

2.2. Task Scheduler (Windows)

For Windows users, Task Scheduler provides a user-friendly interface for managing recurring tasks. You can set triggers based on time or system events.

Steps to Schedule a Python Script Using Task Scheduler:

Open Task Scheduler and select "Create Basic Task."

Follow the wizard to set the task name and trigger (daily, weekly, etc.).

In the action step, choose "Start a program" and point to the Python executable, with the path to your script as an argument.

2.3. Airflow

Apache Airflow is a powerful platform to programmatically author, schedule, and monitor workflows. It allows for complex workflows with dependencies.

Basic Example of an Airflow DAG:

```python
from airflow import DAG

from airflow.operators.python_operator import PythonOperator from datetime import datetime

def update_data():

# Your data update logic here pass

dag            =            DAG('data_update_workflow',
```

```
start_date=datetime(2023,          1,          1),
schedule_interval='@daily')    update_data_task    =
PythonOperator(
```

```
task_id='update_data',
```

```
python_callable=update_data, dag=dag
```

```
)
```
```

### 2.4. Python Libraries

For those who prefer staying entirely within Python, libraries like `schedule` or `APScheduler` can be used to run background jobs at specified intervals.

**Example using the `schedule` Library:**

```python
```python import schedule import time
```

```
def job():
```

```
print("Updating                              data...")
schedule.every().day.at("00:00").do(job)
```

```
while True:
```

```
schedule.run_pending() time.sleep(1)
```
```

## 3. Managing Dependencies and Logging

When automating scripts, it's crucial to handle any potential issues that could arise. Here are some strategies for effective script management:

### 3.1. Handling Dependencies

Make sure that all dependencies are clearly defined in a requirements file (e.g., `requirements.txt`). This ensures
```

that your script will run in optimal conditions, regardless of the environment.

3.2. Logging

Implement logging in your scripts to capture information about each run. This can help you troubleshoot issues. Python's built-in `logging` library makes this straightforward.

Example of Basic Logging:

```python
import logging

logging.basicConfig(filename='data_update.log', level=logging.INFO) def update_data():
```

```python
logging.info("Data update started.")
```

```python
# Your data update logic logging.info("Data update completed.")
```
```

## 4. Error Handling and Notifications

Automating data updates means that your scripts must account for potential errors such as network failures, invalid data, or exceeding execution time. Consider implementing error handling mechanisms.

**Example: Using Try-Except Blocks:**

```python
def update_data():
```

```python
try:
```

```python
# Your data update logic
```

```python
...
```
```

```
except Exception as e:

logging.error(f"An error occurred: {e}")

# Optionally trigger a notification (e.g., send an email)
```
\ \ \

5. Testing and Validation

Before fully automating your data updates, ensure rigorous testing of your scripts to catch any unforeseen issues. This may involve:

Running scripts manually and validating outputs.

Checking edge cases with sample data.

Setting up automated tests using frameworks like `pytest`.

By leveraging tools like Cron, Task Scheduler, Apache Airflow, or simply using Python libraries, you can automate your workflows effectively. Remember to include robust error handling, logging, and thorough testing to ensure that your data updates run smoothly and reliably. With these practices in place, your data will always be fresh and readily available for analysis, driving better decision- making across your organization.

Creating Python-based Data Pipelines

Data pipelines are essential for transforming raw data into a structured format suitable for analysis and insights. Python, with its simplicity and extensive libraries, offers a powerful environment to create robust data pipelines. This chapter aims to guide you through the fundamental concepts and techniques for building Python-based data pipelines.

1. Understanding Data Pipelines

A data pipeline is a series of data processing steps. The input is the raw data collected from various sources—databases, APIs, flat files, etc.—and the output is a refined dataset, often stored in a database or data warehouse, ready for analytics or machine learning. Data pipelines typically consist of the following stages:

Extraction: Collecting data from different sources.

Transformation: Cleaning and converting data into a suitable format.

Loading: Storing the transformed data into a target system. Understanding these stages is crucial for designing effective data pipelines. ## 2. Tools and Libraries

Python offers a rich ecosystem of libraries and frameworks that can assist in constructing data pipelines. Here are some notable ones:

Pandas: A powerful library for data manipulation and analysis.

NumPy: Essential for performing numerical operations and handling large datasets.

Apache Airflow: A platform for programmatically authoring, scheduling, and monitoring workflows.

Luigi: A framework to build complex data pipelines with dependency management.

Dask: Allows scalable and parallel computing for large datasets.

PySpark: A Python interface for Apache Spark,

145

enabling large-scale data processing.

Depending on the complexity of your pipeline, you can choose one or more of these tools to create scalable solutions.

3. Setting Up the Environment

Before diving into pipeline development, ensure you have your Python environment set up. You can use environments like Anaconda or virtualenv to manage dependencies. Install key libraries using pip:

```bash
pip install pandas numpy apache-airflow luigi dask pyspark
```

4. Building a Simple Data Pipeline

Let's build a simple data pipeline that reads data from a CSV file, performs some transformations, and saves it to a new CSV file.

Step 1: Data Extraction

We will start by extracting data from a CSV file using Pandas.

```python
import pandas as pd

def extract_data(file_path):

return pd.read_csv(file_path)

data = extract_data('input_data.csv')
```

```
```

Step 2: Data Transformation

Now, let's clean and transform our data. Assume our data contains a column with missing values, and we want to fill those with the column mean.

```python
def transform_data(data):

# Fill missing values with column means

for column in data.select_dtypes(include=[float, int]).columns: data[column].fillna(data[column].mean(), inplace=True)

return data

transformed_data = transform_data(data)
```

Step 3: Data Loading

Finally, we will save our transformed data to a new CSV file.

```python
def load_data(data, output_file_path):

data.to_csv(output_file_path, index=False)

load_data(transformed_data, 'output_data.csv')
```

Bringing it all together, you can encapsulate the above steps in a function called `data_pipeline`.

```python
```

```python
def data_pipeline(input_file, output_file):

data = extract_data(input_file) transformed_data = transform_data(data) load_data(transformed_data, output_file)

data_pipeline('input_data.csv', 'output_data.csv')
```

5. Error Handling and Logging

Robust data pipelines should include error handling to manage potential issues during processing. You can use Python's `try` and `except` blocks.

```python
def safe_extract_data(file_path):

try:

return pd.read_csv(file_path) except Exception as e:

print(f"Error while extracting data: {e}")
```

Adding logging can also help track the pipeline's activities and troubleshoot issues.

```python
import logging

logging.basicConfig(level=logging.INFO)

def extract_data_with_logging(file_path): logging.info("Starting data extraction...") try:

data = pd.read_csv(file_path) logging.info("Data extraction successful.") return data

except Exception as e:
```

```
logging.error(f"Error during data extraction: {e}")
```
```

## 6. Building More Complex Pipelines

For more complex scenarios, you can utilize frameworks like Apache Airflow or Luigi to manage workflows with dependencies. These frameworks allow you to define tasks, monitor their status, and automate the execution of your data pipelines.

### Example with Apache Airflow:

To create a basic workflow in Apache Airflow:

Install Airflow and initialize the database.

Define a DAG (Directed Acyclic Graph) for the pipeline.

```python
from airflow import DAG

from airflow.operators.python_operator import PythonOperator from datetime import datetime

def extract_data_task():

return extract_data('input_data.csv')

def transform_data_task():

data = extract_data_task() return transform_data(data)

def load_data_task():

transformed_data = transform_data_task()

return load_data(transformed_data, 'output_data.csv')

default_args = { 'owner': 'airflow',

'start_date': datetime(2023, 1, 1),
```
```

```
}
dag = DAG('data_pipeline', default_args=default_args,
schedule_interval='@daily')          extract_task          =
PythonOperator(task_id='extract',
python_callable=extract_data_task, dag=dag)

transform_task = PythonOperator(task_id='transform',
python_callable=transform_data_task,          dag=dag)
load_task          =          PythonOperator(task_id='load',
python_callable=load_data_task, dag=dag)

extract_task >> transform_task >> load_task
```
```
```

As data continues to grow in volume and complexity, mastering these techniques will be vital for data engineers and analysts alike. In the following chapters, we will delve deeper into specialized topics, enhancing our data processing capabilities in Python.

Chapter 10: Data Sets and Performance Optimization In Excel with python

Microsoft Excel is a widely-used tool for data analysis, but as datasets grow larger, performance can become an issue. Fortunately, with the powerful capabilities of Python, we can enhance Excel's functionality and optimize performance for data handling. This chapter will explore various methods to manage extensive datasets in Excel and optimize performance using Python.

10.1 Understanding Excel's Limitations

Excel is a powerful tool; however, it has inherent limitations, particularly when handling large datasets. The following constraints are often encountered:

Row Limits: Excel worksheets can handle a maximum of 1,048,576 rows. For industries dealing with extensive data, this can be a significant limitation.

Performance Slowdowns: As the number of formulas, conditional formatting rules, and data connections increases, Excel may slow down considerably.

File Size Constraints: Large Excel files can be cumbersome to share and open, leading to inefficiencies.

Understanding these limitations is the first step in optimizing performance and implementing effective data management strategies with Python.

10.2 Integrating Python with Excel

Python has gained popularity among data analysts and scientists due to its versatility and efficiency in handling large datasets. You can utilize libraries such as `pandas`, `openpyxl`, and `xlrd` to read, manipulate, and write Excel files seamlessly.

10.2.1 Setting Up Your Environment

To get started, install the necessary libraries using pip:

```bash
pip install pandas openpyxl
```

This will give you the tools you need to read from and write to Excel files while performing complex data manipulations.

10.2.2 Reading Excel Files with Pandas

Using the `pandas` library, you can easily read Excel files into DataFrames for analysis:

```python
import pandas as pd
# Load the Excel file
df = pd.read_excel('data.xlsx', sheet_name='Sheet1')
```

This operation allows you to work with your data in a more flexible environment than Excel, providing greater performance for large datasets.

10.3 Data Manipulation and Cleanup

Before optimizing performance, it's essential to ensure that your dataset is clean and organized. Here are some common steps in data manipulation using pandas:

Removing Duplicates:

```python df.drop_duplicates(inplace=True)
```

Handling Missing Values:

```python
df.fillna(method='ffill', inplace=True)
```

Filtering Data:

```python
filtered_df = df[df['column_name'] > threshold]
```

These steps help in preparing the dataset for further analysis and optimize the processing time. ### 10.4 Performance Optimization Techniques

Once the data is clean, you can implement several optimization techniques to boost performance. #### 10.4.1 Working with Smaller Datasets

If your dataset is too large, consider partitioning it into manageable chunks. You can then process these segments and aggregate results:

```python
chunksize = 10000

for chunk in pd.read_excel('large_data.xlsx', chunksize=chunksize): process_chunk(chunk)
```

10.4.2 Efficient Data Operations

Using vectorized operations and avoiding loops in pandas can drastically improve performance. For example, instead of iterating through rows:

```python
df['new_column'] = df['column1'] + df['column2']
```

This leverages pandas' efficiency in handling operations, resulting in faster execution times. #### 10.4.3 Using Numpy for Numerical Data

For numerical calculations, consider integrating NumPy for its performance benefits:

```python
import numpy as np
df['sqrt_column'] = np.sqrt(df['numerical_column'])
```

NumPy is optimized for numerical operations and can handle arrays with higher efficiency than native Python.

10.5 Exporting Results Back to Excel

After performing the required data manipulations and optimizations, exporting the results back to an Excel file is straightforward:

```python
df.to_excel('cleaned_data.xlsx', index=False)
```

This allows you to leverage Excel's visualization tools, maintaining a familiar interface for end-users. ### 10.6 Conclusion

Optimizing performance when working with large datasets in Excel comes down to understanding the limitations of the tool and utilizing the strengths of Python. By integrating Python with Excel, you can efficiently manipulate and analyze extensive datasets that excel might otherwise struggle with.

Leveraging Python in coordination with Excel can bridge the gap between ease of use and performance capabilities. With `pandas` and other libraries, you can unlock powerful data manipulation techniques while maintaining the accessibility of Excel for presentation and reporting. As datasets continue to grow in scope and complexity, such integration will become increasingly vital for data professionals seeking efficiency and effectiveness in their analyses.

Techniques for Managing Large Data Volumes in Excel with Python

Fortunately, Python offers powerful libraries that can enhance Excel's data manipulation capabilities. This chapter explores techniques to manage, analyze, and visualize large datasets in Excel using Python, enabling users to leverage the strengths of both tools.

1. Understanding the Limitations of Excel

Before delving into specific techniques, it is essential to understand the limitations of Excel when working with large data volumes. These include:

Row Limitations: Excel has a maximum of 1,048,576 rows per sheet. For datasets exceeding this limit, other methods must be employed.

Performance Issues: Files with hundreds of thousands of rows can become sluggish, leading to slow loading times and frequent crashes.

Data Corruption: Large files may become corrupted or difficult to manage, leading to potential data loss.

Understanding these limitations is crucial for deciding when to integrate Python into your workflow. ## 2. Setting Up Your Environment

To start using Python with Excel, you will need a few essential tools:

Python: Install Python on your system. The Anaconda

distribution is highly recommended for its ease of package management and deployment.

Libraries: Install relevant libraries such as `pandas`, `openpyxl`, and `xlrd` using pip or conda. These libraries allow for data manipulation and Excel file handling.

```bash
pip install pandas openpyxl xlrd
```

3. Loading Large Excel Files Efficiently

Loading large datasets into memory is often the first bottleneck in data analysis. Here are techniques to load data efficiently with Python:

3.1 Using Pandas for Chunking

Pandas provides a functionality to read Excel files in chunks, which is especially useful for very large datasets.

```python
import pandas as pd

# Read in chunks

chunk_size = 100000  # Adjust as necessary

chunks = pd.read_excel('large_data.xlsx', chunksize=chunk_size)

# Process each chunk for chunk in chunks:

# Perform operations like filtering or aggregating process_chunk(chunk)
```

3.2 Filtering on Import

158

If you only need specific columns or rows, use the `usecols` and `skiprows` parameters to reduce memory usage.

```python
df = pd.read_excel('large_data.xlsx', usecols='A:C', skiprows=10)
```

4. Data Cleaning and Transformation

Once you load the data into a Pandas DataFrame, you can perform various cleaning and transformation operations.

4.1 Handling Missing Values

Missing data is a common issue in large datasets. You can easily drop or fill missing values using Pandas.

```python
# Drop rows with missing values df.dropna(inplace=True)

# Fill missing values df.fillna(0, inplace=True)
```

4.2 Data Type Conversion

Ensuring that your data types are appropriate is essential for performance. Use functions like `astype()` for conversion.

```python
df['column_name'] = df['column_name'].astype('category')
```

5. Data Analysis Techniques

With properly cleaned data in Pandas, you can perform various analytical operations: ### 5.1 Grouping and Aggregation

You can easily group your data and compute summary statistics.

```python
grouped                                      =
df.groupby('category_column').agg({'value_column':
'sum'})
```

5.2 Time Series Analysis

If your data contains a date or time component, leverage Pandas' powerful time series capabilities.

```python
df['date_column'] = pd.to_datetime(df['date_column'])
df.set_index('date_column').resample('M').sum()
```

6. Visualization of Large Datasets

Once the analysis is complete, visualizing the results is crucial for insights. While Excel has built-in charting tools, integrating Python libraries like Matplotlib and Seaborn can provide greater flexibility and customization.

6.1 Using Matplotlib for Custom Visuals

```python
import matplotlib.pyplot as plt

# Simple plot of grouped data grouped.plot(kind='bar')
```

plt.title('Value by Category') plt.xlabel('Category') plt.ylabel('Total Value') plt.show()

```
```

6.2 Creating Interactive Visuals with Plotly

If you need more interactive capabilities, consider using Plotly.

```python
import plotly.express as px

fig = px.bar(grouped.reset_index(), x='category_column', y='value_column', title='Interactive Bar Chart') fig.show()
```

7. Exporting Processed Data Back to Excel

After your analysis and visualization, you may want to export the results back to Excel for reporting or sharing.

```python
df.to_excel('processed_data.xlsx', index=False)
```

By leveraging Python's powerful data manipulation capabilities alongside Excel, users can overcome the limitations of standard Excel operations when handling large data volumes. The techniques outlined in this chapter—from efficient data loading to advanced analysis and visualization—enable users to manage expansive datasets effectively. As data continues to grow, mastering these tools will empower professionals to make informed, data-driven decisions seamlessly.

Optimizing Python Code for Performance

While its ease of use is one of its most appealing qualities, performance is often a concern when dealing with large datasets in Excel. In this chapter, we will delve into strategies for optimizing Python code specifically tailored for tasks associated with Excel, ensuring that you can work efficiently without being hindered by time-consuming operations.

Understanding the Performance Bottlenecks

Before we dive into optimization techniques, it's crucial to identify the common performance bottlenecks that can arise when interfacing Python with Excel:

I/O Operations: Reading from and writing to Excel files can be slow, especially with large datasets.

Data Structures: Inefficient use of data structures can lead to unnecessary complexity and slow performance.

Looping through Rows/Columns: Python provides numerous powerful functions that should be leveraged instead of manual iteration.

Memory Usage: Large datasets can exhaust memory, leading to slowdowns or crashes.

By understanding these pitfalls, we can then focus on various methods to mitigate their effects. ## Tips for Optimization

1. Efficiently Read and Write Excel Files

Using libraries that are optimized for handling Excel files is paramount. While `pandas` and `openpyxl` are great, they can be slow with large datasets. Here's how you can optimize reading and writing operations:

- **Use the `chunk_size` Parameter**: When reading a large Excel file with `pandas.read_excel()`, leverage the `chunksize` parameter to process the file in smaller, manageable portions.

```python
import pandas as pd

# Reading large Excel file in chunks

for chunk in pd.read_excel('large_file.xlsx', chunksize=10000): process_data(chunk)
```

- **Write DataFrames in One Go**: When dealing with modifications, try to accumulate your results and write them back with a single `to_excel()` call rather than multiple writes.

```python
result_df.to_excel('output_file.xlsx', index=False)
```

2. Use Vectorized Operations

One of the biggest advantages of libraries like pandas is their support for vectorized operations. Instead of using for-loops, which can significantly slow down your code, utilize these built-in functions:

```python
# Instead of this:

for i in range(len(df)):

df['new_column'][i] = df['column1'][i] + df['column2'][i]
```

```
# Do this:
df['new_column'] = df['column1'] + df['column2']
```
```

### 3. Profile Your Code

Before you optimize, it's essential to know where your code is slow. Use profiling tools such as `cProfile` or `line_profiler` to identify bottlenecks in your code.

```python import cProfile import pstats
def main():
# Your code here...
cProfile.run('main()', 'output.stats') p = pstats.Stats('output.stats')
p.sort_stats('cumulative').print_stats(10)
```

4. Optimize Loops and Conditional Expressions

If you must use loops, ensure they are optimized. This includes:

Avoiding nested loops: Try to utilize pandas functions that can handle multiple operations in one go.

Using `apply()` method wisely: Though powerful, `apply()` can sometimes be slower than a vectorized approach. Always check if a vectorized solution exists.

5. Manage Memory Usage

Python's memory management can significantly affect performance. Here are some ways to optimize memory usage:

164
```

Use appropriate data types: Converting data types in DataFrames can help save memory. For instance, change `float64` to `float32` if precision is not an issue, or use `category` for string values that take on a limited number of unique values.

```python
df['category_column'] = df['category_column'].astype('category')
```

Delete unnecessary variables: Free up memory by deleting DataFrames or variables you no longer need using the `del` statement.

6. Parallel Processing

For HPC (High Performance Computing) scenarios, consider leveraging libraries such as `Dask` or `joblib` for parallel processing, especially for tasks that can be executed concurrently.

```python
from dask import dataframe as dd

df = dd.read_csv('large_file.csv')  # Dask will handle chunks internally df['new_column'] = df['column1'] + df['column2'] df.to_csv('output_file-*.csv', index=False)
```

Optimizing Python code for performance while working with Excel files requires a comprehensive understanding of both the limitations of your tools and the best practices of Python programming. By employing strategies such as efficient I/O operations, vectorized computations, memory management, and parallel processing, you can significantly enhance the performance of your data analysis tasks.

Chapter 11: Visualizing External Data in Excel with python

This chapter will delve into how Python can be used to access, manipulate, and visualize external datasets in Excel. By harnessing the power of Python libraries such as Pandas, Matplotlib, and OpenPyXL, we can create visually appealing and informative data presentations that transcend basic Excel functionalities.

11.1 Introduction to External Data Sources

External data can come from various sources, including online databases, APIs, CSV files, or even web scraping. Common formats for data exchange include CSV, JSON, and XML. This versatility allows for the integration of different datasets into our analyses.

11.1.1 Key External Data Sources

CSV Files: Easy to generate and read, CSV files are widely used for data export. Most systems and applications support exporting data in this format.

APIs: Application Programming Interfaces provide a way to retrieve live data from web services. Understanding RESTful APIs is key to harnessing this data.

Databases: SQL databases, NoSQL databases, and cloud-based data solutions allow for complex querying and extensive data handling.

Web Scraping: This technique can collect data from websites that do not provide a direct download feature.

11.2 Setting Up Your Python Environment

Before we get started with data visualization, ensure you

have the necessary Python packages installed. Here's how to set up a basic environment using `pip`:

```bash
pip install pandas matplotlib openpyxl requests
```

Pandas: For data manipulation and analysis.

Matplotlib: For creating static, animated, and interactive visualizations in Python.

OpenPyXL: For reading and writing Excel files.

Requests: For handling API requests efficiently. ## 11.3 Loading External Data into Python

The first step is loading your external data into a Pandas DataFrame. Let's explore how to do this with different data sources.

11.3.1 Reading from CSV

To read a CSV file, use the following code snippet:

```python
import pandas as pd
```

```python
# Load dataset from CSV
data = pd.read_csv('path_to_your_file.csv')
print(data.head())
```

11.3.2 Fetching Data from an API

When dealing with APIs, the `requests` library is indispensable. Below is an example of how to query a JSON API and convert it to a DataFrame:

```python
import requests

# Fetch data from an API
response = requests.get('https://api.example.com/data')
data_json = response.json()

# Convert JSON to DataFrame
data = pd.DataFrame(data_json)
print(data.head())
```

11.4 Data Cleaning and Preparation

Once the data has been loaded, it's essential to conduct a thorough data cleaning process to ensure that it is both accurate and relevant for visualization. This includes handling missing values, removing duplicates, and ensuring data types are appropriate.

```python
# Handling missing values
data.dropna(inplace=True)

# Removing duplicates
data.drop_duplicates(inplace=True)

# Converting data types if necessary
```

169

```python
data['date_column']                                      =
pd.to_datetime(data['date_column'])
```

11.5 Visualizing Data with Matplotlib

Now that the data is clean and ready for visualization, let's explore how to create some graphs. The choice of chart should depend on what insights you are trying to convey.

11.5.1 Creating Basic Plots

A simple line plot can visualize trends over time:

```python
import matplotlib.pyplot as plt

# Basic line plot plt.figure(figsize=(10, 5))

plt.plot(data['date_column'],        data['value_column'])
plt.title('Trend over Time')
```

```
plt.xlabel('Date') plt.ylabel('Values') plt.grid() plt.show()
```

11.5.2 Bar Charts for Comparisons

For categorical comparisons, a bar chart works wonders:

````python # Bar plot

```
categories = data['category_column'].value_counts()
plt.bar(categories.index, categories.values)
plt.title('Category Comparison') plt.xlabel('Categories')
```

```
plt.ylabel('Counts') plt.xticks(rotation=45) plt.show()
```
````

11.6 Exporting Visualizations Back to Excel

Once the visualizations are complete, you may need to save the charts and findings back into an Excel file for reporting or further analysis.

11.6.1 Creating an Excel Workbook

Using `OpenPyXL`, you can create an Excel file and embed your charts within it.

```python
from openpyxl import Workbook

from openpyxl.drawing.image import Image

# Create a workbook and add a worksheet wb =
Workbook()

ws = wb.active

ws.title = "Data Visualization"

# Save the plot to an image file
```

```
plt.savefig('plot_image.png')        img        =
Image('plot_image.png') ws.add_image(img, 'A1')
```

```
# Save the Workbook wb.save('visualized_data.xlsx')
```
```
` ` `
```

This chapter has provided a framework for visualizing external data in Excel using Python. The integration of Python libraries with Excel not only enhances data manipulation capabilities but also offers advanced visualization options. By combining the strengths of Python and Excel, professionals can create compelling and informative reports that can drive informed decision-making.

Creating Dynamic Charts and Graphs from External Data with Python

With Python, we can effortlessly create stunning and dynamic charts and graphs that can adapt to changes in external data. This chapter will walk you through the process of building dynamic visual representations of your data using Python libraries such as Matplotlib, Seaborn, and Plotly. We will also discuss how to pull data from external sources like CSV files, APIs, and databases.

1. Setting Up the Environment

Before diving into data visualization, we need to ensure that we have the necessary tools installed. The key libraries we will use are:

Pandas: For data manipulation and analysis.

Matplotlib: For static plotting and visualization.

Seaborn: For statistical data visualizations based on

Matplotlib.

Plotly: For interactive visualizations. ### Installation

You can install the required libraries using pip:

```bash
pip install pandas matplotlib seaborn plotly
```

2. Loading Data from External Sources

To create dynamic charts, we first need to load data from an external source. In this section, we will cover how to load data from a CSV file and an API into a Pandas DataFrame.

2.1 Loading Data from a CSV File

Pandas makes it simple to read data from a CSV file:

```python
import pandas as pd

# Load the data
data = pd.read_csv('data.csv')

# Display the first few rows of the DataFrame
print(data.head())
```

2.2 Loading Data from an API

For dynamic data, we often need to fetch it from web APIs:

```python
import requests

# Fetch data from an API
```

```python
response = requests.get('https://api.example.com/data')
data_json = response.json()
# Load data into a DataFrame data = pd.DataFrame(data_json)
print(data.head())
```

3. Creating Static Visualizations

Once we have our data loaded into a DataFrame, we can start creating visualizations. Here's how to create basic charts using Matplotlib and Seaborn.

3.1 Using Matplotlib

Matplotlib is versatile for creating various static plots. Here's how to create a simple line chart:

```python
import matplotlib.pyplot as plt
# Create a line chart plt.figure(figsize=(10, 5))
plt.plot(data['date'], data['value'], marker='o') plt.title('Line Chart Example') plt.xlabel('Date')
plt.ylabel('Value') plt.xticks(rotation=45) plt.grid()
plt.show()
```

3.2 Using Seaborn

Seaborn simplifies the process of drawing attractive statistical graphics. For example, creating a bar chart is straightforward:

```python
```
174

```python
import seaborn as sns
# Create a bar chart plt.figure(figsize=(10, 5))
sns.barplot(x='category', y='value', data=data) plt.title('Bar Chart Example') plt.xlabel('Category')
plt.ylabel('Value') plt.xticks(rotation=45) plt.show()
```

4. Creating Interactive Visualizations

For a more dynamic user experience, we can utilize Plotly to create interactive charts. This allows users to hover over points, zoom in, and even share the visualizations.

4.1 Creating an Interactive Line Chart

Here's how to create an interactive line chart with Plotly:

```python
import plotly.express as px
# Create an interactive line chart
fig = px.line(data, x='date', y='value', title='Interactive Line Chart Example') fig.show()
```

4.2 Creating a Dynamic Dashboard

Plotly Dash allows us to create interactive web-based dashboards easily. Here's a basic example of how to set up a Dash app:

```python
import dash
from dash import dcc, html
# Initialize the Dash app
```

```
app = dash.Dash(__name__)
# Set up layout app.layout = html.Div([
html.H1("Dynamic Data Dashboard"), dcc.Graph(
id='dynamic-line-chart',   figure=px.line(data,   x='date',
y='value')
)
])
# Run the app
if __name__ == '__main__':
app.run_server(debug=True)
```

5. Automating Data Updates

To ensure our visualizations reflect the most current data, we can automate data updates. This could involve setting up scheduled scripts or using webhooks to refresh data whenever there is a change.

5.1 Using Cron Jobs (Linux/macOS)

Running a Python script daily to fetch fresh data can be achieved with cron jobs:

```bash
# Open the crontab editor crontab -e
# Schedule the script
0 0 * * * /usr/bin/python3 /path/to/your_script.py
```

Through these techniques, you can enhance your data

analysis and presentation, enabling better insights and decision-making. The world of data visualization is vast and continually expanding, and by leveraging Python's capabilities, you can navigate it with ease and creativity.

Using Python Libraries for Data Visualization

With the rise of big data and analytics, the ability to illustrate findings through graphs, charts, and plots is more important than ever. Python, renowned for its simplicity and versatility, offers a rich ecosystem of libraries that facilitate data visualization. In this chapter, we will explore some of the most popular Python libraries for data visualization, their features, and how to use them effectively to create insightful visuals.

1. Introduction to Data Visualization

Before delving into the libraries, it is vital to understand the principles of data visualization. Effective visualizations can reveal patterns, trends, and outliers in data that might not be immediately apparent through raw data analysis. Key aspects to consider when creating visualizations include:

Clarity: The visual should be easy to read and understand.

Accuracy: Represent the data truthfully, avoiding misleading representations.

Relevance: Focus on the aspects of data that are pertinent to the question at hand.

Aesthetics: A visually appealing chart can enhance engagement and understanding. ## 2. Popular Python Libraries for Data Visualization

In Python, several libraries stand out for their capabilities in data visualization. Here, we discuss some of the most widely-used options.

2.1 Matplotlib

Matplotlib is one of the oldest and most widely-used libraries for plotting in Python. It provides a flexible and powerful interface to create static, animated, and interactive visualizations.

Key Features:

Supports a wide variety of charts such as line plots, scatter plots, bar charts, histograms, and more.

Highly customizable with options for changing colors, line styles, markers, and annotations.

Integrates well with Jupyter Notebook, making it an excellent tool for exploratory data analysis.

Example of Usage:

```python
import matplotlib.pyplot as plt import numpy as np

# Sample Data

x = np.linspace(0, 10, 100) y = np.sin(x)

# Create a Line Plot

plt.plot(x, y, label='Sine Wave', color='blue') plt.title('Sine Wave Example')

plt.xlabel('X-axis') plt.ylabel('Y-axis')

plt.axhline(0, color='black', lw=0.5, ls='--') # Adding a horizontal line
```

```
plt.legend()
plt.grid(True) plt.show()
```

2.2 Seaborn

Seaborn is built on top of Matplotlib and comes with enhanced features for statistical data visualization. It simplifies the process of creating informative and attractive plots.

Key Features:

Built-in themes for aesthetics.

Automatically handles the complexities of statistical graphics.

Functions for heatmaps, violin plots, and categorical data visualizations.

Example of Usage:

```python
import seaborn as sns

import matplotlib.pyplot as plt

# Load an example dataset tips = sns.load_dataset('tips')

# Create a scatter plot with regression line

sns.scatterplot(data=tips, x='total_bill', y='tip', hue='day', style='time') sns.regplot(data=tips, x='total_bill', y='tip', scatter=False, color='red')

plt.title('Tips vs. Total Bill') plt.show()
```

2.3 Plotly

Plotly is a library for creating interactive visualizations. It is widely used for web-based applications and dashboards, allowing users to engage with data dynamically.

Key Features:

Interactivity with zooming, panning, and data point hovering.

Easy to create dashboards with multiple charts.

Support for a wide range of visualization types, including 3D plots.

Example of Usage:

```python
import plotly.express as px

# Load an example dataset df = px.data.iris()

# Create an interactive scatter plot

fig = px.scatter(df, x='sepal_width', y='sepal_length', color='species', title='Iris Sepal Width vs Length')

fig.show()
```

2.4 Bokeh

Bokeh is another powerful library for creating interactive visualizations in web applications. It focuses on enabling the creation of functional and interactive plots.

Key Features:

Capable of handling large datasets efficiently.

180

Tools for adding interactivity such as sliders and dropdowns.

Integrates seamlessly with web applications.

Example of Usage:

```python
from bokeh.plotting import figure, show from bokeh.io import output_notebook

output_notebook() # Create data
x = [1, 2, 3, 4, 5]
y = [6, 7, 2, 4, 5]
# Create a new plot
p = figure(title="Simple Line Example", x_axis_label='X-axis',          y_axis_label='Y-axis')          p.line(x,          y, legend_label="Line", line_width=2)
# Show the plot show(p)
```

2.5 Altair

Altair is a declarative statistical visualization library based on Vega and Vega-Lite. It allows users to generate visualizations by defining the visualization in terms of the data.

Key Features:

Simplified syntax for complex visualizations.

Built on a foundation of best practices for data visualization.

Automatically chooses the best visual encoding for the

provided data.

Example of Usage:

```python
import altair as alt import pandas as pd
# Create a DataFrame data = pd.DataFrame({
'x': [1, 2, 3, 4, 5],
'y': [5, 3, 6, 2, 4]
})
# Create a simple scatter plot
chart = alt.Chart(data).mark_circle().encode( x='x',
y='y'
).properties(title='Altair Scatter Plot')
# Display the chart chart.display()
```

3. Choosing the Right Library

When deciding which library to use for a specific visualization task, consider the following:

Complexity of Visualization: For simple plots, Matplotlib or Seaborn may suffice. For interactive needs, Plotly or Bokeh would be better suited.

Aesthetic Requirements: If aesthetics are a priority, Seaborn and Plotly provide enhanced visual appeal.

Interactivity: For web applications or dashboards needing dynamic user interaction, choose Plotly or Bokeh.

Statistical Visualization: If you work heavily with

statistics, Seaborn and Altair offer robust functionality tailored for that purpose.

From creating simple line charts to intricate interactive plots, mastering these libraries will significantly enhance your ability to present data compellingly. As you develop your visualization skills, remember the key principles of clarity, accuracy, relevance, and aesthetics to ensure that your insights are communicated effectively. With practice, you will be able to choose the right tools and techniques to create impactful visual stories that resonate with your audience.

Chapter 12: Error Handling and Troubleshooting

Python, with its robust libraries such as `pandas` and `openpyxl`, provides a powerful toolkit for interacting with Excel files. However, when working with external data sources, errors can occur due to various reasons, such as connectivity issues, file corruption, or unexpected data formats. This chapter focuses on effective error handling techniques in Python when dealing with Excel external data sources, enabling developers to create resilient and user-friendly applications.

12.1 Understanding Common Errors

Before diving into error handling strategies, it's important to understand some of the common errors that may arise while working with Excel files:

FileNotFoundError: This error occurs when the specified Excel file does not exist in the provided path.

ValueError: Raised when trying to convert an incompatible data type, especially when performing operations on data read from Excel.

pd.errors.EmptyDataError: This error occurs when attempting to read from an Excel file that is empty or does not contain valid data.

pd.errors.ParserError: Raised when the data read from the Excel file is malformed or cannot be correctly parsed by the `pandas` library.

ConnectionError: This error arises when there are issues with connecting to the external data source, such as a database or data API.

Understanding these common pitfalls is the first step toward robust error handling. ## 12.2 Structuring Error Handling with Try-Except

The `try-except` block in Python allows developers to catch errors at runtime rather than having the entire program crash due to an unhandled exception. The basic structure is as follows:

```python
```python try:
# Code that may raise an exception

df = pd.read_excel('data_source.xlsx') except FileNotFoundError:

print("Error: The specified file was not found.") except ValueError as ve:

print(f"ValueError: {ve}") except pd.errors.EmptyDataError:

print("Error: The Excel file is empty.") except pd.errors.ParserError:

print("Error: Could not parse the data from the Excel file.") except Exception as e:

print(f"An unexpected error occurred: {e}")
```
```

In this structure, each type of exception can be handled separately, allowing for more granular control over the error handling process.

12.3 Logging Errors

When dealing with external data sources, it's crucial not just to handle errors gracefully but also to log them for later analysis. Implementing logging allows developers to keep track of what went wrong during execution and aids in debugging:

```python
import logging

# Configure logging
logging.basicConfig(filename='error_log.log', level=logging.ERROR)

try:
    df = pd.read_excel('data_source.xlsx')
except Exception as e:
    logging.error(f"An error occurred: {e}")
    print("An error occurred. Please check the error log for more details.")
```

By logging errors, you create a persistent record that can be reviewed, helping identify patterns in failures or inconsistencies in external data sources.

12.4 Implementing Retry Logic

In certain cases, particularly when dealing with network connectivity issues, it may be beneficial to implement a retry mechanism. This allows the program to attempt to establish a connection several times before failing definitively. The `tenacity` library makes it easy to implement retry logic:

```python
from tenacity import retry, stop_after_attempt

@retry(stop=stop_after_attempt(3))                    def
read_excel_file(file_path):

return pd.read_excel(file_path)

try:

df = read_excel_file('data_source.xlsx') except Exception
as e:

logging.error(f"Failed to read the Excel file after several
attempts: {e}") print("Could not read the file after
multiple attempts.")
```

In this example, the `read_excel_file` function will
automatically retry reading the Excel file up to three times
before raising an error, potentially resolving transient
issues.

12.5 User-Friendly Error Messages

Lastly, while technical logging is useful for developers,
end-users will benefit from clear and understandable error
messages. Errors should be communicated in such a way
that users can comprehend the issue and, if possible, take
corrective measures:

```python
try:
df = pd.read_excel('data_source.xlsx')
```

```
except FileNotFoundError:
```

print("It looks like we can't find the file 'data_source.xlsx'. Please check the file path and try again.") except pd.errors.EmptyDataError:

print("The file is empty. Please fill it with data and attempt again.")

```
```

Offering guidance along with error notifications improves user experience and reduces frustration when issues occur.

Effective error handling when working with external data sources is essential for building robust Python applications. By understanding common errors, utilizing `try-except` blocks, logging errors, implementing retry logic, and providing user-friendly messages, developers can make their applications not only more resilient but also more intuitive for users. The strategies discussed in this chapter will enhance your toolkit for managing external data sources effectively, allowing you to focus on leveraging data rather than merely surviving the pitfalls associated with it.

Common Errors in Data Excel Integration

However, the process of integrating data into Excel— whether from databases, cloud services, or other spreadsheets—can be fraught with challenges. This chapter aims to identify and explore common errors encountered during data Excel integration, providing insights and best practices for mitigating these issues.

1. Incorrect Data Formats

One of the primary errors encountered when integrating data into Excel is the misuse of data formats. Data comes in various types such as text, numbers, dates, or currencies, and improperly formatted data can lead to significant issues in analysis. For instance, when importing dates from an external source, Excel may recognize them in a different format (e.g., DD/MM/YYYY instead of MM/DD/YYYY). This can result in misinterpretation of the data, leading to incorrect calculations and erroneous conclusions.

Best Practice: Always check the data formats before performing integration. Use Excel's text-to- columns feature or the DATEVALUE function to convert and format data correctly.

2. Missing or Incomplete Data

Data integration often involves merging data from multiple sources. A frequent complication arises when one or more datasets have missing or incomplete data entries. This can cause errors during data analysis, reporting, and visualization. For example, if a dataset pertaining to sales figures is missing entries for a specific month, it could skew trends and result in misleading interpretations.

Best Practice: Implement data validation checks using Excel's built-in data validation features and regularly audit data sources to ensure completeness before integration.

3. Duplication of Data

The presence of duplicate records is another common error that can emerge during data integration. Duplicates can arise from merging multiple datasets that contain overlapping information. These duplicates can distort analysis results, leading to inflated metrics and flawed decision-making.

Best Practice: Use Excel's "Remove Duplicates" feature to clean datasets, and incorporate unique identifiers or keys wherever feasible to facilitate a more controlled integration process.

4. Misaligned Data Structures

When integrating data from heterogeneous sources, misalignment in data structures can be a significant roadblock. For example, merging data where one dataset uses a different naming convention for the same attribute (e.g., 'Customer_ID' vs. 'ID_Customer') can lead to integration errors and complicate analysis.

Best Practice: Establish clear data mapping guidelines before integration. Create a data dictionary that outlines the fields in each source and standardizes naming conventions.

5. Formula and Reference Errors

Excel users often employ formulas and references to analyze integrated data. However, errors may arise due to broken links, circular references, or incorrect formula inputs. These errors can lead to inaccurate results and create inconsistencies in reports.

Best Practice: Validate formulas regularly and conduct thorough testing after integration. Use the "Evaluate Formula" tool in Excel to troubleshoot and identify errors in complex formulas.

6. Incomplete Data Refreshes

For those integrating live data from external systems, incomplete or failed refreshes can lead to using outdated or inaccurate data in reports. This is particularly relevant for organizations relying on real-time data to inform decision-making processes.

Best Practice: Establish a systematic process for data refreshes and make use of Excel's data connection settings to ensure that updates are timely and comprehensive.

7. Lack of Documentation

Finally, one of the often-overlooked errors in data integration is the lack of adequate documentation. When data sources and integration methods are not documented, it becomes challenging to troubleshoot issues, replicate the integration process, or onboard new team members.

Best Practice: Maintain comprehensive documentation that outlines the data sources, integration techniques, transformation processes, and any encountered issues. This can serve as a valuable reference point for future integration efforts.

Data integration in Excel can significantly enhance analytical capabilities and decision-making. However, it comes with its own set of challenges. By being aware of common errors—including data format issues, missing data, duplication of records, misaligned structures, formula errors, incomplete refreshes, and lack of documentation—users can adopt proactive strategies to mitigate these problems.

Error Resolution Techniques In Python Excel External Data Sources

These errors can arise from various issues, including file format incompatibilities, data type mismatches, connection problems, and incorrect data handling practices. This chapter aims to explore common errors encountered when working with Excel files via Python and discusses viable techniques for resolution.

Understanding Excel Data Integration

Before diving into error resolution techniques, it is essential to understand the context in which errors may arise. Python provides several libraries for interacting with Excel files, the most popular being:

Pandas: Ideal for data manipulation and analysis.

OpenPyXL: Useful for reading and writing Excel 2010 xlsx/xlsm/xltx/xltm files.

xlrd/xlwt: Historically used for reading/writing older Excel files but now largely superseded by OpenPyXL and Pandas.

While these libraries allow seamless integration with Excel, several points of failure can lead to errors, especially when dealing with external data sources.

Common Errors and Their Resolutions ### File Not Found Errors

Symptoms: When attempting to open an Excel file, a `FileNotFoundError` is raised.

Resolution Techniques:

Check File Path: Ensure that the file path is correct.

Use `os.path.isfile()` to confirm that the file exists at the specified location.

```python
import os
file_path = 'data/myfile.xlsx' if os.path.isfile(file_path):
# proceed to open the file else:
print(f"File not found: {file_path}")
```

Use Absolute Paths: Instead of relative paths, use absolute paths to avoid ambiguity in file location. ### Excel File Format Errors

Symptoms: Errors like `InvalidFileException` can occur when you try to open non-Excel files with Excel libraries.

Resolution Techniques:

Validate File Format: Ensure that the file is indeed in the correct Excel format. You can use file type assertions based on extensions.

```python
```

```python
import os
if not file_path.endswith(('.xlsx', '.xls')):
    raise ValueError("File format is not supported.")
```

Convert Files: If necessary, convert incompatible files using Excel or an external converter tool before processing.

Data Type Mismatches

Symptoms: Data type errors often surface during data manipulation, such as when attempting to perform numerical operations on strings.

Resolution Techniques:

Data Cleaning: Before performing operations like calculations, clean the data using `pandas` to convert strings to numbers where applicable.

```python
df['numeric_column'] = pd.to_numeric(df['numeric_column'], errors='coerce')
```

Error Handling: Implement try-except blocks to catch and handle `ValueError` exceptions during type conversion.

```python
try:
df['numeric_column'] = df['numeric_column'].astype(float) except ValueError as e:
```

194

```
print(f"Error converting data: {e}")
```

Connection Errors

Symptoms: When attempting to connect to external databases or services, you might encounter `ConnectionError`.

Resolution Techniques:

Check Network Connectivity: Ensure that your network connection is active.

Validate Credentials: Ensure that credentials and connection parameters (hostname, port, username, password) are correctly set and not expired.

Use Connection Pooling: For frequent database access, use a pooling library like `sqlalchemy` to manage connections efficiently.

Handling Missing or Corrupted Data

Symptoms: Encountering missing data or corrupted cells can lead to NaN values in DataFrames or errors during processing.

Resolution Techniques:

Fill Missing Values: Use `DataFrame.fillna()` to handle NaN values.

```python
df.fillna(0, inplace=True)  # Replace NaN with 0
```

Data Validation: Before processing, validate the integrity of your data.

```python
if df.isnull().values.any():
```

print("Warning: Missing values found")
```

```

Log and Report Issues: Implement logging to keep track of data quality issues for future analysis. ### Exception Handling in Data Processing

When working with external data sources, unexpected errors can happen at any stage of data processing. It is crucial to employ effective exception handling strategies to ensure robustness.

Resolution Techniques:

Try-Except Blocks: Use these blocks around critical code sections to catch exceptions gracefully.

```python try:
```

Load data

df = pd.read_excel(file_path) except Exception as e:

print(f"An error occurred: {e}")
```

```

Logging: Use Python's built-in logging library to log errors instead of printing them, which can help in debugging.

```python import logging
```

logging.basicConfig(level=logging.ERROR)
logging.error("Error message: %s", str(e))
```

```

By understanding the potential points of failure, implementing error-checking measures, and employing robust exception handling practices, you can enhance the reliability of your data processing workflow significantly. As the landscape of data continues to evolve, staying updated on best practices and tools will empower you to manage external data sources confidently and effectively.

```

```

Chapter 13: Security Considerations for Data Integration

Organizations are required to exchange data to optimize processes, enhance decision-making, and foster innovation. However, this exchange introduces numerous security challenges that must be addressed to protect sensitive information and ensure compliance with regulatory requirements. This chapter examines critical security considerations in data integration, best practices for securing data flows, and strategies to mitigate risks.

The Vulnerability Landscape

Data integration facilitates the movement of information between disparate systems, applications, and databases. As data flows across networks, it is exposed to a range of vulnerabilities:

Data Breaches: Unprotected data can be intercepted during transmission, leading to unauthorized access and breaches.

Insider Threats: Employees or partners with legitimate access may misuse or leak sensitive data during integration processes.

Malware and Ransomware: Malicious software can infiltrate systems, compromising or encrypting data during integration.

Insecure APIs: Application Programming Interfaces (APIs) expose integration points that can be exploited if not properly secured.

1. Understanding Risks Associated with Data Integration

To safeguard data integrity, organizations must perform a thorough risk assessment to understand the vulnerabilities inherent in their integration processes. Risk assessment can help identify potential threat vectors and the specific types of data that are at risk. Key areas of focus include:

Data Sensitivity: Evaluate the nature of the data being integrated—personal, financial, proprietary, or sensitive data requires more stringent controls.

Integration Methods: Analyze the methods used for integration (batch processing, real-time data streaming, etc.) to determine distinct security considerations and risks for each.

Third-party Partnerships: Understand the security posture of any third-party service providers involved in the integration process, as their vulnerabilities can directly affect your organization.

Best Practices for Securing Data Integration

To mitigate the risks associated with data integration and ensure that sensitive data remains protected, organizations should adopt the following best practices:

1. Data Encryption

Data should be encrypted both in transit and at rest. Encryption transforms the data into an unreadable format, ensuring its confidentiality even if intercepted. Organizations should implement standard encryption protocols (such as AES for data at rest and TLS for data in transit) to secure data flows.

2. Access Control and User Authentication

Strict access controls should be enforced to restrict data access to authorized personnel only. Implementing role-based access control (RBAC), multi-factor authentication (MFA), and regular audits of access logs can minimize the risk of insider threats and unauthorized access.

3. API Security

APIs serve as integration points, and securing them is crucial. Use authentication mechanisms, such as OAuth or API keys, and apply rate limiting to prevent abuse. Regular vulnerability assessments and penetration testing of APIs can identify security gaps and potential exploits.

4. Data Masking and Tokenization

Sensitive data should be masked or tokenized during the integration process to prevent exposure. Data masking replaces sensitive data with fictitious data, while tokenization substitutes sensitive elements with non-sensitive equivalents, safeguarding privacy without losing functionality.

5. Monitoring and Logging

Implement comprehensive logging and monitoring mechanisms for all integration activities. These logs can provide insight into data access patterns, helping detect any anomalies that may indicate a breach. Regularly reviewing logs can assist in compliance audits and responsiveness to security incidents.

Compliance and Regulatory Frameworks

Organizations operating in regulated industries must adhere to various compliance frameworks that dictate data protection requirements. Familiarity with these regulations, such as the General Data Protection Regulation (GDPR), Health Insurance Portability and Accountability Act (HIPAA), and the Payment Card Industry Data Security Standard (PCI DSS), is essential. Implementing data integration processes that align with these regulations not only enhances security but also mitigates the risk of legal repercussions.

Incident Response Planning

No matter how robust security measures are, the potential for a data breach always exists. Therefore, organizations must develop a comprehensive incident response plan that outlines steps to take in the event of a security breach during data integration. This plan should include:

Identification of potential data breaches.

Immediate response protocols to contain and assess the breach.

Communication strategies for stakeholders, customers, and regulatory bodies.

Review and update processes to learn from incidents and improve security measures.

As organizations increasingly rely on data flows across applications and systems, addressing vulnerabilities through best practices, compliance frameworks, and incident response planning is critical.

Securing Data Connections and Handling Sensitive Data

As organizations increasingly rely on Excel to analyze and share vast amounts of data, it's essential to ensure that these external data sources are accessed securely. Python, with its powerful libraries and can streamline this process while simultaneously safeguarding sensitive data. This chapter will explore strategies and best practices for securing data connections to external sources when working with Excel in Python.

1. Understanding the Data Landscape

Before diving into security measures, it's important to understand the types of data and sources you may be working with. Excel can connect to several external data sources, including:

Databases: SQL Server, MySQL, PostgreSQL, and others.

APIs: RESTful and SOAP APIs that deliver JSON or XML data.

Flat Files: CSV, JSON, and Excel files on network drives or cloud storage.

Each of these data sources presents unique security challenges, and recognizing these is the first step toward formulating a secure approach.

2. Securing Database Connections

When connecting Python to a database to pull data into Excel, it's paramount to implement secure connection practices, as database credentials are often the keys to sensitive information.

2.1 Use Connection Strings Securely

When establishing a connection to a database, use a secure connection string. Here are some best practices:

Environment Variables: Store sensitive information like username and password in environment variables rather than hard-coding them in scripts. Use Python's `os` module to access these variables.

```python
import os
import psycopg2

db_user = os.getenv("DB_USER") db_password = os.getenv("DB_PASS") connection = psycopg2.connect(
    dbname="your_database",                    user=db_user,
    password=db_password, host="localhost"
)
```

Encryption: Use Secure Sockets Layer (SSL) connections to encrypt the data being sent to and from the database. This can typically be enabled in the connection string.

2.2 Role-based Access Control

Employing role-based access control (RBAC) can further enhance security by providing users with the minimum level of access necessary to perform their job functions. This minimizes risks associated with compromised credentials.

```sql
CREATE ROLE limited_user LOGIN PASSWORD 'securepassword'; GRANT CONNECT ON DATABASE your_database TO limited_user;

-- Add further permissions as necessary
```

3. Securing API Connections

APIs are another common method for pulling external data. Securing these interactions is equally important.

3.1 Authentication and Authorization

API Keys: Use API keys that are generated specifically for your application, and ensure they are stored securely (e.g., in environment variables).

```python
import requests
api_key = os.getenv("API_KEY")

response = requests.get("https://api.example.com/data", headers={"Authorization": f"Bearer {api_key}"})
```

OAuth2: For APIs that require more robust authentication, consider using OAuth2. This allows the adoption of token-based authentication, which can provide additional security.

3.2 HTTPS Protocol

Always use HTTPS rather than HTTP when making requests to ensure that data is encrypted during transmission.

4. Handling Flat Files

When working with flat files such as CSV or Excel files, securing the data involves measures at both the file and transmission levels.

4.1 Secure File Storage

Ensure that any files containing sensitive information are stored in secure locations with restricted access.

Encryption: Consider encrypting the files at rest and controlling access to them. Python libraries like

`cryptography` can be useful here.

```python
from cryptography.fernet import Fernet

key = Fernet.generate_key() cipher = Fernet(key)

# Encrypting data

cipher_text = cipher.encrypt(b"My super secret data")
```

```
# Decrypting data
plain_text = cipher.decrypt(cipher_text)
```

4.2 Secure File Transfer

When transferring files, consider using secure protocols like SFTP or SCP that encrypt data during transit to prevent eavesdropping.

Securing data connections in Python when dealing with Excel external data sources is not just a good practice—it's a necessity. By implementing sound security measures such as using environment variables, applying encryption, ensuring role-based access, and using secure communication protocols, organizations can significantly mitigate risks.

Best Practices for Data Privacy and Compliance

As businesses collect, store, and process vast amounts of personal data, it is essential to implement best practices that adhere to privacy regulations such as the General Data Protection Regulation (GDPR), the California Consumer Privacy Act (CCPA), and other local laws. This chapter explores effective strategies for ensuring data privacy and compliance using Python, one of the most widely-used programming languages for data manipulation and analysis.

1. Understanding Data Privacy and Compliance ### 1.1 Key Concepts

Data privacy refers to the proper handling, processing, storage, and dissemination of personal information. Compliance means adhering to relevant laws and regulations that govern data privacy. Understanding these concepts is critical for any application or service that handles personal data.

1.2 Relevant Regulations

GDPR: A regulation in EU law on data protection and privacy for individuals within the European Union.

CCPA: A California law that enhances privacy rights and consumer protection for residents of California.

HIPAA: A US law that provides data privacy and security provisions for safeguarding medical information.

2. Importance of Compliance in Data Privacy

Failing to comply with data privacy regulations can result in hefty fines, legal issues, and reputational damage. Implementing data privacy practices is not just about meeting legal requirements; it is also about building trust with your users and maintaining a sustainable business model.

3. Best Practices for Data Privacy and Compliance in Python ### 3.1 Data Minimization and Purpose Limitation

Principle: Collect only the personal data necessary for the purposes specified.

Use Python libraries like `pandas` to analyze data and determine what is necessary before collection.

Example:

```python
import pandas as pd
```

```python
# Read data
data = pd.read_csv('user_data.csv')
# Filter out unnecessary columns necessary_data = data[['user_id', 'email']]
```

3.2 Anonymization and Pseudonymization

Principle: Anonymize or pseudonymize data to reduce the risk of exposure.

Use Python libraries like `Faker` for generating synthetic data, which is useful in testing environments.

```python
from faker import Faker fake = Faker()
# Generate fake user data
fake_users = [{'user_id': i, 'email': fake.email()} for i in range(100)]
```

3.3 Secure Storage and Transmission

Principle: Store data securely and ensure it is transmitted safely.

Utilize encryption methods such as `Fernet` from the `cryptography` library for securely storing sensitive information.

```python
from cryptography.fernet import Fernet
```

```python
# Generate a key
key = Fernet.generate_key() cipher_suite = Fernet(key)
# Encrypt data
encrypted_data = cipher_suite.encrypt(b"Sensitive Data")
```

Use `HTTPS` for APIs and web services to ensure encrypted communication channels. ### 3.4 User Consent and Rights Management

Principle: Obtain user consent clearly and provide easy mechanisms for them to manage their data rights.

Create a user interface that allows users to opt-in or opt-out of data collection explicitly.

Use Python's Flask or Django framework to build APIs that enable users to manage their data preferences.

```python
from flask import Flask, request, jsonify

app = Flask(__name__)

@app.route('/consent', methods=['POST']) def manage_consent():
user_data = request.json
# Process consent based on user_data
return jsonify({"status": "Consent updated"}), 200
```

3.5 Data Auditing and Monitoring
Principle: Regularly audit data handling practices and

monitor for breaches.

Use logging frameworks like `logging` in Python to maintain records of data access and modifications.

```python
import logging

logging.basicConfig(filename='data_access.log', level=logging.INFO)
def access_data(user_id):
    logging.info(f"Data accessed for user: {user_id}")
    # Access data for the user
```

3.6 Training and Awareness

Principle: Regularly train your team on data privacy concepts and compliance requirements.

Use Python scripts to automate reminders or distribute educational resources related to data privacy through email libraries such as `smtplib`.

Ensuring data privacy and compliance is an ongoing responsibility that requires a proactive approach. By integrating best practices into your Python applications—from data minimization and secure storage to user consent and regular auditing—you pave the way for a robust data privacy framework. Remember, effective data management not only helps in compliance but also fosters trust with your users, setting the foundation for long-term success in a data-driven world.

Conclusion

In this book, we have embarked on a comprehensive

journey through the integration of Python with Excel and various external data sources. We began by exploring the fundamental concepts of working with Excel files using popular libraries such as Pandas and OpenPyXL. Through practical examples, we learned how to read, manipulate, and write data, transforming raw information into actionable insights.

As we delved deeper, we uncovered the importance of connecting Python with different external data sources, including databases like SQL and NoSQL, web APIs, and CSV files. These integrations empower data analysts and scientists to harness a myriad of datasets, providing a more holistic view for decision- making processes.

Throughout the chapters, we demonstrated various techniques to streamline data processing, automate repetitive tasks, and visualize data effectively. The practical exercises and real-world scenarios illustrated how you can elevate your Excel capabilities by leveraging Python's extensive libraries.

In conclusion, the synergy between Python and Excel opens up a world of possibilities for data analysis and management. As you continue to explore these tools, remember that practice is key. The examples provided in this ebook serve as a foundation upon which you can build your skills and customize solutions that fit your specific needs.

We encourage you to experiment with the methods outlined, explore additional libraries, and stay curious about the evolving landscape of data science. Armed with the knowledge you've gained, you are now well- equipped to take on data challenges with confidence and creativity.

Thank you for joining us on this enlightening journey through Python and Excel. May your data endeavors lead to insightful discoveries and impactful results!

Biography

Bryan Singer is a seasoned authority in the realm of Singer machines, bringing years of hands-on experience and an unparalleled depth of knowledge to his readers. With a background steeped in the intricate workings and history of Singer sewing machines, Bryan has become a trusted name for enthusiasts and professionals alike who seek to master these iconic devices.

Bryan's journey with Singer machines began in his early childhood, sparked by a fascination with the mechanics of his grandmother's vintage Singer. This early passion evolved into a lifelong dedication, leading him to delve into every aspect of these machines, from their historical significance to the latest technological advancements. His expertise is not just theoretical but deeply practical, having restored countless machines to their former glory and assisted numerous individuals in troubleshooting and enhancing their Singer experiences.

Beyond his specialization in Singer machines, Bryan is an avid coder with a love for Python, web application development, and web development. His technical prowess extends to creating innovative solutions with Python, particularly in the realm of Python Excel, where he merges his technical skills with his meticulous attention to detail. This unique blend of mechanical and digital expertise positions Bryan as a versatile and dynamic author.

Glossary: Python Excel External Data Sources

This chapter serves as a glossary, providing clear definitions and explanations of essential terms and concepts that bind Python, Excel, and external data sources together. Understanding these terms will equip you with the vocabulary and insights to harness the full potential of Python in working with Excel.

1. Python

Definition: Python is a high-level, interpreted programming language known for its readability and versatility. It supports various programming paradigms and is extensively used in data analysis, machine learning, web development, automation, and more.

Context: In the realm of Excel and data manipulation, Python offers libraries like `pandas`, `openpyxl`, and `xlrd` that facilitate data extraction, transformation, and loading (ETL) processes.

2. Pandas

Definition: Pandas is an open-source data analysis library for Python designed for manipulating numerical tables and time series data. It provides data structures like DataFrames and Series to enable efficient data handling.

Context: When working with Excel files, pandas simplifies reading and writing operations, data cleaning, and transformation, making it a go-to library for data analysts.

3. DataFrame

Definition: A DataFrame is a two-dimensional, size-mutable, and potentially heterogeneous tabular data structure with labeled axes (rows and columns). It is a primary data structure in pandas.

Context: DataFrames are excellent for holding data imported from Excel sheets and allow for intuitive data manipulation and analysis.

4. openpyxl

Definition: openpyxl is a Python library used for reading and writing Excel (xlsx) files. It supports formatting, charts, and features specific to Excel.

Context: This library is invaluable when you need to interact with modern Excel files directly, enabling users to create, modify, and extract data from Excel spreadsheets.

5. xlrd

Definition: xlrd is a Python package used to read data and formatting information from Excel files, specifically older Excel file formats (xls). It is essential for accessing the data contained in these legacy files.

Context: Although its use is declining with the prevalence of xlsx files, xlrd remains useful for maintaining compatibility with older systems.

6. External Data Sources

Definition: External data sources refer to any data originating outside of the main database or application environment, which can be accessed and analyzed, such as CSV files, databases, APIs, web

scraping, and more.

Context: Python provides the capability to pull in data from various external sources, allowing for richer analysis and reporting within Excel.

7. ETL (Extract, Transform, Load)

Definition: ETL is a data processing framework that involves extracting data from various sources, transforming it into a suitable format, and loading it into a destination (like a database or data warehouse).

Context: In conjunction with Python, ETL processes enable analysts to gather data from multiple Excel files and external databases for comprehensive data analysis.

8. CSV (Comma-Separated Values)

Definition: CSV is a simple file format used to store tabular data, where each line corresponds to a data record and each field within the record is separated by a comma.

Context: Python's ability to read and manipulate CSV files is crucial in times when converting Excel data or interfacing with other data storage methodologies.

9. API (Application Programming Interface)

Definition: APIs are sets of rules and protocols that allow different software applications to communicate with one another. They can expose data endpoints for external access.

Context: Python's ability to integrate with APIs allows you to pull data into Excel from various online sources, such as social media, weather data, or financial data.

10. Data Cleaning

Definition: Data cleaning is the process of identifying and rectifying errors or inconsistencies in data to improve its quality.

Context: Proper data cleaning with Python is essential before importing data into Excel, as it ensures accurate analysis and visualization.

11. Visualization

Definition: Visualization refers to the graphical representation of data and information. It helps communicate data-driven insights through charts, graphs, and dashboards.

Context: Libraries like `matplotlib` and `seaborn` in Python facilitate data visualization, allowing you to create visual representations of Excel data for clearer interpretation.

With this glossary as a reference, you will be well-equipped to navigate the dynamic landscape of data analysis and manipulation, utilizing Python's powerful capabilities to enhance your work with Excel spreadsheets and external datasets. As you progress further in your journey, remember that the seamless connection between these elements will significantly enrich your analytical capabilities and decision-making processes.

www.ingramcontent.com/pod-product-compliance
Lightning Source LLC
LaVergne TN
LVHW051326050326
832903LV00031B/3388